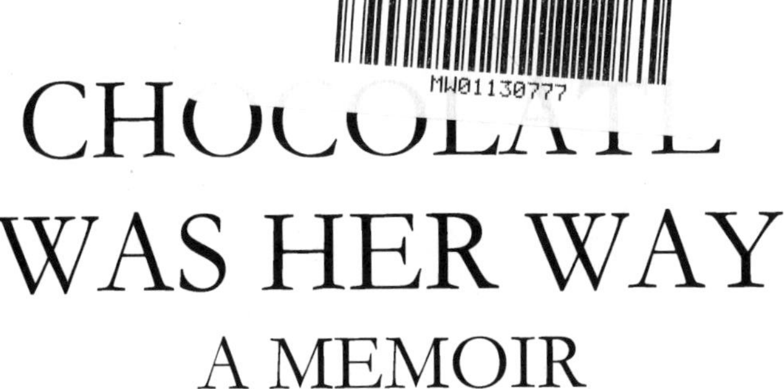

CHOCOLATE WAS HER WAY

A MEMOIR

Margaret Mott

ISBN: 10-1545487308
ISBN-13:978-1545487303

Dear Michelle

Thank you so much
for your interest in
my story

Margaret :)

DEDICATION

Dedicated to Noel and Samuel Douglas - my dream

And to Linda, Cassandra and Mitchell - my reality

CHOCOLATE WAS HER WAY

1966
pregnant
hidden
in the basement
sweet sixteen

Everyday
my mother brought me chocolate
no discussion
ever
I gave my baby to strangers

Reunited
after 27 years
I realized
no one
forced me

I was being
the best mother
I could be
and
chocolate was her way

CHAPTER 1

TORONTO FEBRUARY 20 1966

NO ONE HAD prepared me for the pain. No one.

No one warned me about the sudden rush of warm liquid gushing down my legs. No one.

I watched, in horror, the pool forming on the black and white tiles at my feet. Something had gone terribly wrong. "Mom" She didn't come.

I bunched my flannelette nightgown tight between my legs while I reached to tear off a wad of toilet paper and stuffed it between my legs.

Opening the bathroom door, I called out, "Mother."

Asleep in the bedroom next door, she didn't respond. "Mom." I called louder.

I crept to my parent's bedroom door and opened it as quietly as I could. Leaning close to her ear, I nudged my mother's arm and whispered, "Mom, wake up."

She stirred, her blue eyes fluttered for a moment then focused on my hands clutched between my legs and the deepening stain. "Oh dear." Her voice was filled with fear. "Oh dear, oh dear."

"Shhh." I held my fingers to my lips. My father grunted in his sleep.

"He has to drive." She pushed against his shoulder. "Walt, it's time."

"What the hell's going on Elaine?" My father turned towards us. When he saw me holding myself, he said, "Shit," and pushed the covers back. He sat up resting against the veneer headboard for a moment before slipping his feet into checkered slippers. His striped pajamas were held up at the waist with a string, The powerful smell of stale alcohol and cigarettes clung to him and made me want to vomit. How could my mother sleep night after night with those vile odors?

Mom was reaching for her pink housecoat. Her platinum hair was mussed from sleeping and her cheeks appeared redder than usual. She moved towards the dresser and patted down her hair in the rounded mirror, "Margie, we have to get you to the hospital right away. Just wear a coat over your nightie. There is no time to dress. You can't give birth here."

Her strained face revealed that she considered this a serious concern. After all, she had given birth to me on the same bathroom floor, sixteen years earlier. She had told me the story many times.

It was the summer of 1949. She thought she had to go to the bathroom but I was born minutes later. She stretched out with me on the tile floor waiting for the doctor to arrive. Even

though he had visited our home weekly to play bridge, on the day I was born, he had trouble finding our house. Later my mother learned, he had started taking barbiturates during World War II to boost his energy while working long hours. Addicted, he continued his drug abuse after the war.

The doctor finally arrived and cut the umbilical cord, leaving us on the bathroom floor, he went into the narrow kitchen to make a cup of coffee. Mom recounted how she followed him and thought she needed some Ex-Lax hidden on the top shelf, out of reach from my six year old brother, Doug who was dancing on the front lawn and singing, "I has a baby sister. I has a new baby sister."

A neighbour called my father's office and as the story goes, Dad arrived at the hospital before us and hollered blue murder when they told him that was no one with his wife's name had been admitted. He was still insisting his wife had just given birth to a daughter when we were wheeled past him on a stretcher.

Now sixteen years later, my parents were in a panic to get me to the hospital before the baby came.

The February temperatures hovered well below freezing, leaving the roads icy as we drove. Each slippery turn made me clutch my monstrous stomach as I regurgitated the taste of my last meal. My father kept taking his eyes off the road to look anxiously at me as though I would give birth right there on the front seat of our Valiant.

"Christ, I don't know how to deliver a goddamn baby." He muttered as he pushed his glasses up to his forehead and rubbed his hazel eyes. The whites had become quite red. A growth of salt and pepper whiskers sprouted unattended on his chin. At 59, his hair was still primarily black with only the occasional strand of gray turned a steel color from the Brylcream which slicked it tight to his skin. But now it was unruly from constantly running his fingers over his forehead and through his hair as he drove.

There were few cars on the road and the freezing rain forced my father to drive slower than usual. He avoided the freeway because of the inclement weather, taking Kingston Road to St. Clair, leaving the suburbs behind. When we covered the miles and reached downtown Toronto, the streetcar tracks and muddy rutted roads forced him to slow even further.

"Jesus, Elaine, why didn't we just take her to Scarborough General?" Dad's gravelly voice cracked as he spoke.

"You know why, Walter", her voice was defensive, "It's close to the clinic and no one will recognize her at The Wellesley."

"Leave her alone, Dad," I shouted.

My mother never stood up for herself. She was a cautious woman. Cautious with money, cautious in making friends, cautious in business. Some people might consider my

mother reserved but I felt she was apologetic and insecure and I hated that quality. These past few months however, I appreciated her ability to hide my secret behind her stoic façade.

When he was happy, my father spent money on us extravagantly which made Mom fret openly about money. But when he drank, watch out. If Mom said anything he found disagreeable, wham, his anger erupted violently. I would disappear whereas Mom always appeared on the verge of bursting into tears. The next day, hung over, he would be all sugary. But in our house, we constantly walked on eggshells.

I let out a scream as another contraction violated my body.

My father turned towards me, his face white, "Shit." He pounded the steering wheel and reached for his cigarettes. "We should never have taken this chance. She could have it right here." He coughed up phlegm loudly and rolled down the window to spit it out before handing me the package. I took one and lit it for him.

He gestured for me to keep it and light him another but I shook my head so he took the cigarette and inhaled deeply. Smoke filled the car.

He glanced at me cradling my stomach and **let out a long sigh before turning his attention back to the slippery road.**

Oh my God, I thought. My father is really upset. I'm not the only one suffering here. **A memory of him pushing me as a**

little girl in his wheelbarrow and how much fun we had together working in his garden, then falling asleep with my head on his lap, exhausted each night. ***I feel I lost him years ago. I'm so ashamed for letting him down and now things will never be the same.***

Dad's voice brought me back to the car, "You had her at home for Christ's sake and we almost didn't make it to the hospital for Jeff."

He was right. My mother popped out her babies almost without warning. My brother was nearly born on the same bathroom floor as I was. Thirteen years after she had me, my mother barely made it to the hospital with my kid brother. She swore that she might have even slept through his birth if someone hadn't called to wish us a Happy New Year. She made it to the hospital just in time and was still conscious when she heard the nurse on the phone announcing the time of Jeff's birth to the newspaper, making him the first baby born in Toronto in 1963.

Now, glancing at my three year old brother in the backseat, I prayed we would reach the hospital in time. At least I hadn't given birth in that tiny bathroom with the toilet that constantly overflowed. And we would have been forced to call our local doctor, defeating the purpose of hiding these past months.

A metallic taste permeated my mouth which happened every time I clenched my teeth so I pushed open the side vent, inhaling the brisk night air.

"Don't catch a cold, Dear." My mother warned.

I leaned my head against the cold window and watched my face in the side view mirror. The breeze blew my hair off my face. I used to be so proud of the soft golden locks and brushed it faithfully one hundred strokes a day trying to look like Sandra Dee in her last movie, That Funny Feeling. My heart throbbed when Bobby Darin sang to her. Now, looking at my image, my ears poked through the limp strands, greasy from infrequent washing. My home cut bangs clung against my forehead, which glistened with sweat. As the baby grew, I was frightened to shower or bath too often. My mother constantly reminded me how my grandmother had fallen in the bathtub and used a cane the rest of her life.

I stared hard at my reflection, fascinated by the faint image staring back through the frosted glass. Street lights flashed by, lighting my face. I could see the sixty pounds I had gained in the puffy cheeks. Even the simplest exercise, climbing the steps from the basement, had exhausted me. My eyes looked puffy. I felt so much older than sixteen. A deep line was beginning to form between my eyebrows. My eyes glistened green. 'Your eyes are blue when you're happy and green when you're sad', my boyfriend used to tell me. I bit my

lip and exhaled against the cold glass, watching as my image disappeared into the frost.

The bulk of my body took up the entire space between my seat and the glove compartment. My breasts ached with their heavy weight.

"Ahhhhhh," I clutched my belly and stretched fleshy arms to grasp the dashboard as we skidded along the icy streets.

"Holy shit, Maggie." Dad yelled as he watched me writhe in pain.

"Shush." Mom said. "You'll wake Jeff."

I glanced at my baby brother stretched out on the back seat beside my mother, sleeping soundly. Driving was always the best way to get him to sleep. Mom or I had often packed him into the car late at night and driven around until he drifted off.

Another wave of contractions ripped across me and I tried unsuccessfully to moan quietly. Mom leaned forward and clenched my shoulder. She had insisted on sitting in the back because it was easier for her to get into the back of the two door car. "Oh dear, oh dear," she repeated over and over while patting my shoulder.

She wore her heavy camel colored coat wrapped tight around her bulky frame as she hugged herself in the back seat. Her lips were tight and red broken blood corpuscles covered cheeks deeply lined from years of stress.

As we drove through Rosedale, I surveyed the gracious homes we passed by. Homes similar to the ones Mom's sisters lived in. Stone mansions with stairs leading up from the kitchen to the servants quarters and another *Gone With the Wind* sweeping staircase in the entranceway where a lady could descend in a flowing gown. I wonder if my mother thought of her relatives as we passed and longed for the happier days of her childhood, but she didn't speak.

I imagined dark wood-paneled parlors designed just for music where she told me the family would sing around the piano every Friday night after opulent dinner parties These homes twinkled in the snow like a fairy tale. I longed to live with any one of my aunts.

Turning back to face the road, I watched nervously as Dad zigzagged a little each time he looked over at me. His long fingers gripped the steering wheel. They were tobacco stained and multicolored oil paint clung under rugged bitten fingernails. Brown age spots had begun to color the backs of his hands. He drove through a puddle of slush, which sprayed over a lone pedestrian on the sidewalk. The guy yelled at us but Dad didn't notice, his eyes fixed on the slippery road.

"Are we almost there?" I asked.

"Soon," my mother answered patting my shoulder.

I observed the soot-colored snow shoveled five feet high and remembered the Jamaican women I met once who told me about immigrating to Toronto and being shocked and

disappointed at the filthy snow plowed high. All of her life she had received Christmas cards from her family with pictures of sparkling winter wonderlands. I could imagine her disappointment. I pushed my body higher so I could see the pure white snow, the woman had expected, glistening on the lawns behind the gray mounds.

Finally, Dad pulled into the circular drive of Wellesley Hospital. "You go with her, Elaine. I'll wait here."

Mom started to say something but Dad glared at her. Please don't get him started, I thought. I couldn't bear another argument.

I pushed opened the car door and carefully climbed out of the car and waited as my mother pushed my seat forward to stand beside me. "My poor baby," she whispered clinging to me in the cold air as whispy snowflakes swirled around us. The faint smell of Chanel Number 5 lingered on her cheek. I buried my face in her thick winter coat, feeling her large body tremble. "There isn't much I can do," she explained. "And," her eyes darted towards the car, "you know how much your Dad hates hospitals."

I followed her eyes towards my father who was setting my small overnight bag on the sidewalk. Was he hunched or had the six-foot giant of my childhood shrunk? He glanced my way and wiped his damp cheek. Was it a tear drop or just a melted snowflake? His eye glasses were too fogged to tell.

"Your father does love you very much," she said as she got back in the car.

"Yeah, right."

In daylight, I was sure Mom would have driven alone and stayed with me. A strong wind blew my long hair in my face. Ice particles formed on my nose hairs. I turned my back to block the icy air and pulled my coat tighter around the bulk of my middle. "It's okay, Mom, go." White flakes dusted my eyelashes and tears blurred my vision as I watched my mother return to the car. She pressed her flushed face against the frosted window as they drove into the winter storm. I waved goodbye.

The wind slowed for a moment and a silence set in as I watched the snow drift casually onto the steps of the hospital. It was almost midnight and with little traffic, there was a softness to the world. I closed my eyes and enjoyed breathing the frosty air deep into my lungs. It felt good to be outside, unknown and without the frazzled looks of my mother monitoring my every move or my father averting his eyes when I struggled to sit. Another contraction consumed me and I grabbed the railing to steady myself. When it passed, I forced my heavy legs to move and enter the emergency ward. I had never been in a hospital before, not even to visit someone.

After I filled out the paperwork, a nurse escorted me to a small room with curtains across the doorway. It was windowless with bleak gray walls and just enough space for the

stretcher. She handed me a green hospital gown. "The opening goes at the back".

Sweaty, I wiped my face on the drab gown. It smelled of disinfectant. Other odors - ether, cleaning fluid, medicines and the stench of dirty bedpans, offended my nose but there was no escape.

"Ahhhhhhhhhhhhhhhhhh" Did I really scream that loud?

The nurse scolded me. "It's far too early. The real pain hasn't begun." she said "It'll be hours yet."

Foreign noises escaped involuntarily, followed by peace for a moment as my body relaxed between spasms. I was embarrassed being such a nuisance to the staff. Behave, I demanded of the child I had become.

It should have been a time for immense joy, but the day I gave birth to my daughter was the loneliest, most miserable day of my life.

Besides, I'd already complained enough.

My own scent mixed in - the foul scent of sweaty underarms, the bad egg scented dampness between my legs. I wondered who had last worn the hospital gown. Was the stain on the front old blood? Had the last person died in it? Or were these gowns kept in the maternity ward and only used to bring new life into the world?

"It's time to get you ready," a nurse interrupted my thoughts as she slipped in and pulled the curtain closed.

Strands of dark hair hung out from beneath her starched white cap and blocked her face as she rolled in a table holding a small basin of water, scissors and a razor laid out beside a washcloth faded from over bleaching.

"What are you going to do?" I whispered.

"I've got to shave you." she looked towards me revealing a tired face, her eyes hidden by thick glasses.

"What do you mean?" I asked drawing my legs tight and stretching the green gown under my thighs.

Lines tightened her brow, "The doctor has to see in order to work, now, doesn't he?" She patted my hand and smiled slightly but her tone was harsh, hardened I suspected, by years of dealing with difficult patients like me. "Lie back now so I can get at you."

Humiliated, I allowed her to pull my crossed ankles apart. I turned my face towards the wall and clenched my teeth, swallowing the metallic taste filling my mouth.

For twelve hours I laid on the cot, afraid, lonely and crying over the spasms, before they finally wheeled me into the delivery room where two nurses were busy setting up the equipment. One placed my feet into stirrups and said in a saccharin voice. "It'll be over soon." She adjusted the bright lights overhead pulling them towards my widespread legs.

The two women straightened as a doctor I didn't recognize from the clinic, hurried into the delivery room. The second nurse, a small frail looking woman rushed to hand him

rubber gloves. He barely glanced at her as he pulled them on then reached for a long needle and held it high, flicking it. He smiled as he walked towards me. "This will help you with the pain."

He nodded towards the nurses. The smaller one stepped over and placed her hands under my left side, "Turn to your side so the doctor can give you the epidural." I must have looked as terrified as I felt because she added, "It won't hurt and soon you'll feel much better."

"Come on," the nurse pushed impatiently. I turned and clenched my eyes shut waiting for the needle to penetrate. Even with my eyes closed, the lights overhead created a surreal wave of brightness.

Next, the doctor pulled a white mask over his face and positioned himself between my legs. I wanted to close them before this stranger but the nurse pulled them further apart.

"We need you to help us." The doctor said. "Keep pushing as long as you are able." He nodded for his tools, "Dilated 8 centimeters." He smiled in my direction, "Your baby will be out soon. Take a deep breath and push."

I did as instructed but part of me preferred to suffer rather than thrust this new life into the world. I wanted to keep him or her inside where I could feel the kicks and dream of a life together. But even with the medication, I feel the contractions urge my baby to leave me.

"Keep pushing. The head is out. Just a little longer." The doctor encouraged. "Hand me the forceps. She's not pushing hard enough. I may need to help."

One nurse wiped my forehead with a cool cloth and chanted, " Push. Push."

I tried hard not to look at the mirror above me. I could see something pink between my legs and the doctor with metal prongs suspended over it. I could taste blood where I bit my lip. "Mommy", I whispered as my arms grasped at the air for a hand to hold.

I heard my baby's high pitched wail.

"It's a girl." Nurse Saccharin announced.

"Can I see her?"

She hesitated, looking towards the doctor. "I don't think I'm supposed to."

"Go ahead," he said in a caring tone. "You have a beautiful baby girl. Healthy. Ten fingers and ten toes. She's perfect."

She was pink. Her eyes were squeezed closed and her tiny mouth protested loudly. As I reached to touch her tiny fingers, the nurse snatched her away.

"I want my baby."

The doctor nodded. "It's okay. Just for a moment."

Just for a moment. I glared at the doctor but my anger softened, as soon as I turned to my baby and studied her tiny features. Her little hand clutched at my finger. I yearned to

hold her but when I held out my hands, the nurse pulled back then turned and left while cooing gently.

"Go to sleep now." The doctor advised. "You've worked hard."

SLEEPING, WAKING, EMPTY. Everything ached. It's the stitches, the nurse told me.

"I want to see my baby."

"I'm sorry. We can't bring her," each nurse confirmed. "Orders from Children's Aid."

Drifting in and out of consciousness, I yearned for her. For five days, I watched the other mothers in my ward feed their babies and listened to them coo. I stared at the ceiling to avoid observing their happiness. The scent of so many flower bouquets permeated the room. The pungent odor of large white lilies stunk like a weed and made me sneeze. Families visited and fussed over the mothers and babies. I buried my head in my pillow but their laughter filled my ears even after visiting hours ended or when I tried to sleep. The other mothers regarded me with sympathy and I could hear them whispering amongst themselves. All I received was a phone call from my mother each day with some excuse for why she couldn't visit - Dad needed her at his shop or the car broke down.

That night, I realized that one of the nurses had been a few years ahead of me in high school. As she cleared my uneaten dinner tray, I grabbed her hand, "Please don't tell anyone." She frantically scanned the room then pretended she didn't know me. "Please." She nodded and hurried out, never coming into my ward again.

Boy I've really screwed up, I thought. There goes my dream of going to university. Can't go without finishing high school and I can never show my face there again.

THE SECOND DAY when they allowed me to walk, I stood in front of the nursery with the tiny cots lined up staring at my daughter. I moved from foot to foot, shifting my weight to stop the pain of the stitches until one of the staff grabbed my hand and lead me back to my bed.

On day four, before I was to be released the following morning, I heard a familiar voice, "Margie."

"Aunt Joy," I pulled the bedcovers to my chin. "What are you doing here?"

She leaned down and kissed my forehead. Her soft gray curls tickled my face as her perfume, a floral scent, enveloped me. She was short, like my mother, but slim. She had always seemed interested in me.

My Aunt Joy was the fifth oldest in Mom's family of seven siblings, five girls and two boys. One brother, Uncle Edmond, had died in his early thirties. No one would ever tell

me what happened to him. My mother was the youngest and still considered to be the baby in the family.

Most of Mom's sisters seemed to belong in the Victorian era – straight laced and overly well mannered. But Aunt Joy, even though she lived in a mansion on the same street as her sisters - except Mom of course - never seemed stiff or formal. And she never lectured me the way Aunt Ester or Aunt Margaret did. They were always telling me to help my mother more, sit up like a lady, don't cross your legs.

"I wanted to see my niece," she paused, " and the baby."

Instantly, my eyes teared. "You do?"

"Yes, I do."

"I don't know if they'll let us."

She took my arm and helped me out of the bed. "It's okay. I've arranged it."

We went to the nursery window and a nurse held up my baby girl Aunt Joy laced her arm around me and pulled me close. "She's beautiful."

I leaned into her and let the months of sadness spill out. She simply held me and repeated, "there, there." My hair was filthy and needed washing. I felt embarrassed that it must stink of sweat. After a few moments, I straightened and wiped my damp cheeks on the hospital gown. Aunt Joy tapped the glass and made kissing sounds towards my baby.

"She is beautiful, isn't she?" I agreed.

My aunt pushed my straggly blonde hair behind my ear, her fingers lingered for a moment on my wet cheek, "Yes, just like her mother."

My heart leaped at being acknowledged as my baby's mother. I looked up at my Aunt Joy's damp, red eyes and collapsed against her shoulder where we clung to each other and cried.

"I want to keep her."

My aunt took my hands in hers and held them tightly, "Of course you do, but it's better for the baby."

"I know, I know besides Mom won't," sobs choked off the rest. The sound of my gasping for air echoed off the faded hospital walls. Nurses and visitors slowed and stared at us, whispering.

"Don't be mad at your mother. She hasn't had an easy life." my aunt insisted.

"She should leave Dad. I would never put up with his bullshit."

"Your father loves your mother."

"Yeah, sure."

"When you're older, you'll understand marriage isn't always easy," Aunt Joy said.

"I may never get married."

"Yes you will, Dear. You'll find a wonderful man, I'm sure."

"I want my daughter." I pleaded.

"You'll have lots more babies. She'll go to a lovely home. Look at our Bertie. His mother did the right thing and we're so blessed to have him." My aunt had two natural daughters but had adopted a son.

My face lit up. Maybe Aunt Joy would adopt her. I watched closely as she smiled at my baby. What if I asked? My shoulders dropped, recalling that Children's Aid wouldn't allow it because then I would know her whereabouts.

I must have made a sound because my aunt turned expectantly, "Yes?"

I gazed into her eyes, wishing I had the nerve to ask. "Nothing. I didn't say anything."

She hugged me tightly and whispered, "Whoever gets your baby will be very lucky indeed."

My aunt and I never again discussed my situation but I was grateful someone in my family had acknowledged me and my baby.

***

Looking back now, I can hardly believe this is about me. It's like a story I've read about some another young girl. How could I have known back then that as my life unfolded, the most horrible thing that ever happened to me; turned out to be the best.

CHAPTER 2

THE SUMMER HAD started out great. Friends from school wanted to hang out with me because I was cool. I was old enough to drive. I spent the summer transporting giggling girls in Mom's old Vauxhall through Yorkville where we hung out with hippies in coffee houses to listen to folk music. We'd circle around the block over and over, amusing ourselves by placing bets on whether the person with hair worn to their waist, walking on the sidewalk ahead of us was a boy or a girl. The streets were packed with young people from all over North America. Haight-Ashbury types or Rochdale, the Toronto equivalent of the San Francisco hippie hangout. Guys would make lewd gestures. I remember one who called out, "Wanna fuck girls?" while the girl with him laughed and yelled, "Go home to mommy." Real hippies didn't live in the suburbs and drive their mother's car. Real hippies wore Salvation Army clothing, love beads and let their hair grow. Some even walked barefoot.

One weekend that summer, I talked to a guy selling radical newspapers on the street and I took him home with me because he didn't have a place to sleep that night. Mom and Dad welcomed him warmly even though he was quite weird with tattered jeans, a dirty tee shirt and no shoes. My mother

actually asked him if there was a public cupboard in Yorkville where the hippies could park their shoes. Dad took him shopping for a new shirt and underwear then offered him money if he would trim the front hedge. The boy agreed but said he had to return the unsold newspapers first otherwise he wouldn't get paid. My father paid him in advance and of course we never saw him again. I was surprised at my dad's generosity to a total stranger. Dad looked more hurt than angry. I had been caught up so often in defending my mother that I had never noticed his soft side before.

Another weekend, I went out with the guy who worked at the Grab Bag, a variety store in Yorkville. I had talked to him the previous weekend when I bought cigarettes. He asked me to meet him the following Sunday for dinner which I did. He was acting really strange, dozy and faraway. He told me that he dropped acid the night before. I freaked and asked, "why would you do that? It'll burn your stomach out." He laughed so hard, he sat down on the sidewalk and virtually rolled over. How was I to know that acid was LSD? I quickly realized we weren't meant for each other.

Sometimes, my girlfriends and I would chip in for parking and pay the cover charge at a coffee house where we'd sip a creamy cappuccino, slowly to make it last. We'd listen to aspiring folk singers with guitars on their laps, in cluttered rooms with rickety tables, the surfaces carved on by previous patrons. We tried to disguise our suburbaness by inhaling

deeply on cigarettes in a room clouded with smoke. Yeah, man, we belonged.

Rarely could we afford the more affluent clubs like the Riverboat or The Purple Onion where up-and-coming talent like Carly Simon or Joni Mitchell would perform. Mostly, we'd circle the block while I played, Ray Charles, "Let's Go Get Stoned" on my portable 45 record player which sat on the front car seat with the volume cranked up. We'd sing along as though we were hip and got stoned all the time when in reality, we'd never even tried drugs. I'd heard rumors about kids, some who even attended my school, who did crazy things on LSD, like jumping off the Bloor Street bridge thinking they could fly. But my crowd was pretty straight. Besides, booze got us in enough trouble.

We drank and made out in the school playground at night. The first time I tried alcohol, four girls shared a mickey of lemon gin and another of straight gin. We passed the bottles around until they were empty. I spent the rest of the night puking, with snot shooting out my nose. I thought I'd die and promised God I would never drink like that again if he would only let me live until morning. I can't tolerate the tart smell of gin to this day.

AT FIRST I tried to pretend it wasn't really happening. Every morning I'd run to the bathroom and check for blood while swallowing back nausea. At night, I would kneel beside my

bed, clasping my hands together and pray for my period. I swore to never again complain about the stomach cramps and promised to be a good girl. Twice I lowered my body and sat on the top step leading to the basement then bumped my way to the bottom. I had heard that could induce a miscarriage. But in truth, as frightened as I was, I held each stair and slid slowly.

Weeks passed and my period didn't start.

SOCIETY WAS GOING through a sexual revolution. Boys slept with as many girls as possible, yet still believed they would marry a virgin. And the girls I knew, including myself, pretended to be virgins while hoping not to get caught. We were experimenting with sex and pretending not to, having been taught that sex before marriage was forbidden. None of us wanted to be known as a slut, a name certain to spread around school if anyone found you were going all the way.

I'd hear my parents arguing. My father would yell at my mother that she was too lenient. My father knew what boys wanted and I shouldn't be allowed the freedom my mother granted. Well, he was right about what the boys wanted and now he would discover I had wanted it too.

How can I explain the shame involved in being single and pregnant in 1965? I realize now that there were many of us. Girls got pregnant and quickly married the father,

pretending the baby was premature when it was born. There were a lot of seven month babies back then. Everyone supported the lie, agreeing that firstborns were always premature. Teenage boys were forced to marry young girls they got 'into trouble'. It didn't matter that these young parents were babies themselves and not in love with each other. It was the honorable thing to do to avoid the girl's otherwise social ruin – as if no one knew the real reason they got married.

I remember one girlfriend from high school, who got pregnant and married the father. His parents bought them a house, which bordered on the school grounds. At recess, I would talk to her though the wire fence as she sat in the yard holding her baby. At first, she pretended she was happy playing 'grown up' but it quickly turned sour when her husband went to work and she felt stuck at home as nursemaid to a kid who whined constantly for attention. She would stand at the fence watching her school friends laugh and play together, while ignoring the baby crawling at her feet. Once, I watched the baby puke up a yellow slime, then wail for her mother who glared at it. She picked it up and held it at arms length, vomit dripping from it's chin onto a soiled yellow sleeper. She turned to me and screamed in a voice that could be heard across the baseball field, "I hate my fucking life."

Eventually my friend left her husband and her child. I heard that she went wild, doing drugs and prostituting herself

for money to travel and indulge in her new passion for skydiving. Her in- laws were left to raise the baby.

Marrying my baby's father felt like death to me.

If you didn't marry the guy, you hid. That's just the way things were. Girls disappeared, then re-appeared months later. No one discussed the disappearance. At least, not publicly. Society agreed to pretend nothing had happened.

Suicide seemed my only alternative. I sat looking at the bottle of aspirins for several minutes before pouring the contents into my palm. There must have been twenty pills. I couldn't fathom taking that many, even to kill myself. In my family, we needed to practically be on our deathbed to take two aspirins, so I poured back all but five. With a dramatic flare, I popped them into my mouth and washed them down with a glass of milk. Then I waited. I lay on my bed and observed my body. Nothing happened. My breasts, already large for my age, rose and fell normally. I expected to become tired but was wide awake. I could hear Hoss Cartwright and Little Joe on the television. My parents were watching Bonanza, their regular Sunday night program. Finally, at eleven, relieved, I got up and peed. What did I know about committing suicide? I was just a kid. Besides, as bad as things were, I was more afraid of dying than of facing my parents.

A FEW DAYS later, I was sitting at the pull out cutting board in the kitchen, peeling carrots from my father's garden. It was a narrow room with no space for a table.

"Mom."

"Yes, Dear." She was standing at the sink so she turned off the water and set down the last potato she was washing. "I love the taste of freshly picked vegetables. Don't you? So much better than store bought."

"Mmm." My thoughts were elsewhere.

"You never help your Dad in the garden anymore. You used to like it so much."

Angrily, I chopped down hard on the carrots to cut them into individual circles.

"That was a long time ago. I was just a kid."

She wiped her hands on the frilled sunflower apron. "I guess you're too busy with school now. Starting grade eleven in September. Hard to believe you're so grown up."

I felt a chill and shuddered involuntarily.

"Poor dear," Mom smiled. "Are you nervous?"

"About school, I think I want to take a year off."

"What?" Her face filled with alarm. "You can't mean that. Don't let your father hear you say such a thing. You must have an education. All the women in our family went to university."

"You can't afford it and I'm not going to win a scholarship like Doug, so what's the point?"

She squeezed my hand with hers. They felt rough against my skin. Pulling the footstool beside me, she sat her large frame down wearily. "What on earth would you do?"

"I'd find something."

"It's out of the question." She stood, "As long as you live at home, you'll attend school and that's final."

Her tone was so definite, it surprised me. She rarely ordered me to do anything. I watched as she smoothed her sleeveless shift with the multicolored flower pattern, then spooned instant coffee into a chipped cup before plugging in the electric kettle. I shrugged and resumed chopping carrots, dropping the subject for the moment. I observed my flushed reflection in the shine of the tea kettle on the counter and thought if my period didn't begin soon, I'd start to show. Then she would figure it out, and so would everyone else.

SETTING THE TABLE, I recalled how Mom always called it the silver and so did I until I was corrected once by one of my aunts, "It's only called the silver, Dear, if it's really silver. Otherwise, it is referred to as cutlery." To Mom it would always be the silver. At least these days she only set out a knife and fork, not like the rows of cutlery when I was young and got in trouble because I couldn't remember what each utensil was for.

"You need to learn these things," Mom would tell me.

"Why?" I used to ask.

"In case you ever have dinner with the Queen."

That evening I could barely eat. The overpowering smell of thawed salmon which had been left in a freezer too long and reduced for quick sale, hurled my stomach. I wish she had made macaroni and cheese but that was Tuesday's meal. Sundays we ordered Chinese takeout. Meatloaf Mondays. Wednesdays were usually whatever was on special, like today's salmon. Often it was a cheap cut of lamb or foods with smells that lingered.

"Stop playing with your food." Dad interrupted my thoughts and waved his fork. "And finish your dinner."

"I'm not hungry."

"Just finish what's on your plate, Dear." My mother urged. "Think of the starving children in India."

"Then wrap it up and mail it to them."

Dad finished his drink in one gulp then hammered the table. The sudden pounding startled my mother and me. Everything shook and I grabbed my plate with one hand and my glass with the other.

"Alright, alright." I said and shoved a large fork full of salmon into my mouth. Feeling it rise back up, I swallowed hard praying I wouldn't throw up at the dinner table.

Mom shifted nervously and leaned forward to upright the crystal salt and pepper shakers. Her face lit up as she

pointed to the two watercolors above the table. "Don't you love the new paintings?"

"Where'd they come from again?" I asked, happy for the change of subject.

"Your Aunt Maybn and Uncle Basil gave them to us when they moved from the big house into the apartment."

"Why would I want someone else's painting?" My father said. "They should have given them to one of your other sisters."

Mom held her napkin in front of her mouth as she answered, "My sisters have plenty of pictures. They have some of yours hanging too, Walt. Mabyn thought you'd enjoy them. The watercolors are so different from your oils. And they're probably the most valuable thing we own, next to the piano."

Dad grunted and poured another rum from the bottle on the floor beside him, topping it with Diet Coke.

I shifted and touched the polished surface of Mother's baby grand from my place on the piano bench. At dinner time, the bench was pulled up to the table as an extra chair. The piano monopolized the small room, leaving only enough space for a table with two leaves, which had to be put down after meals to allow enough room to walk from the hall through the dining room to the living room.

She noticed and said, "It's not too late to take lessons. You won't have to…"

"I know, I know. I won't have to do the dishes or feed the cat if I take a lesson every night."

Mom laughed. She had been offering me the same deal for years.

"Maybe I will take lessons this winter."

Mom's face lit up. "Really?"

Might as well, I thought, I'll have lots of time if I'm forced to quit school.

She stood up, "Perhaps I'll clean the ivory."

After we cleared the table, I helped her with a soft cloth dipped in milk. Mom lovingly polished each key. She seldom played the piano anymore but it was her proudest possession - a wedding gift from her mother twenty-three years earlier and already at least fifty years old at that time. 'The top of the line Heintzman', she had reminded me over and over for as long as I could remember.

Her face lit up when I asked, "Mom, would you go for a walk?"

She glanced at the dirty dishes then back towards me, smiling, "They can wait." She took off her floral apron revealing chocolate colored slacks. "I can walk in these." She picked up the blue tube from the window sill and squeezed a small amount of Nivea on to her chapped hands and rubbed it in as she walked into the front hall. The smell of the hand cream assaulted my nose. I used to love the smell of Nivea but

now it made me want to vomit as I had been doing for the past few mornings.

Turning the small crystal knob on the windowed door into the living room, she poked her head through and spoke to my father, "Dear, I'm going for a walk with Margie." He sort of grunted from the couch. "You don't mind do you?"

Waving his hand, "Shhhh, Lestor B. Pearson is talking on the news."

Mom turned towards me and smiled, "He's listening to the Prime Minister, guess he won't miss me." Resting her hands on my shoulders, she said, "It's been a long time since we've had a walk together." The front door was open to allow in a cool evening breeze. Pushing the screen open, we descended the bright red steps and crossed the lawn to the far corner where a hole had been worn through the hedge by all of us too lazy to walk around the curved driveway. As we pushed through the branches, a neighbour called out a greeting from her front lawn across the street.

Mom, of course had to stop and explain that Margie had asked her to go for a walk and it was such a lovely evening, how could she resist. I shifted uncomfortably from one foot to the other as I listened to my mother ask about each of her several children. They operated a turkey farm. As my mother chatted, my mind wandered to the summers when I was five through nine and my parents forced me to go every spring and scrape last years hardened turkey shit off their pens in time for

the arrival of a new batch of chicks. I hated it. The thought of the crusted pens made my stomach hurl. Back then, my parents received a fresh slaughtered turkey every Thanksgiving, Christmas and Easter for my efforts. I got a bottle of Coke.

Mom grabbed my hand finally and we began our walk towards the end of the street passing the dirt drive leading up to the gravel pit.

"I heard a rumor that the Japanese couple who own the gravel pit are selling. Imagine, just a few short years ago we were all so afraid of the Japanese. They are lovely people and their son is such a nice young man. The son was your first kiss, remember?"

I remembered. I was ten and we played spin the bottle at my first party with boys and girls.

"I heard a whole new subdivision will be built there." Mom continued, "So many new homes on our street. Soon the city will eliminate any feel of the country."

I nodded as she rambled on about each house we passed. "Remember when you and Anita were six and you tried to walk to the moon? It was a full harvest moon and I guess it did feel like it was right at the top of the street but your father and I were scared to death when we realized you had wandered off at night. Thank heavens you only got as far as the Roberts and they phoned me to come and get you. You had forgotten all about the moon and were engrossed in eating

pizza instead." She patted her stomach, "Sorry you inherited my addiction to food rather than Dad's metabolism." She glanced at my waist, "You are going to have to start watching it a little." My heart kerplunked and I could feel my face and ears redden.

We continued to the end of the street to The Bush. The Bush as everyone referred to it was where Highland Creek, a tributary of the Don River, cut a rugged valley through our suburb. We stopped at the top overlooking a cliff to the valley below. Mom took a deep breath, "Lovely."

It was that magical hour before sunset when each tree stood pronounced by long shadows. A pink hue coated the scene. It was my favourite time of day but this evening, my pending confession blurred my vision.

Taking my hand, Mom led us towards the steep trail at the right, which descended through the forest to the stream below. She let go as we were forced to climb down in single file. Clutching branches for support, she chattered away about family - a cousin who had become engaged and some funny thing my baby brother had done that day. She pointed out a brown squirrel and made a clicking sound to attract its attention.

We reached the bottom and stood in a clearing beside the natural swimming hole where I had spent many days as a child. I knew I had to get it over with quickly or I'd chicken

out again. With a deep breath, I blurted out, "Mom, I'm in trouble."

She understood immediately. She grabbed a branch and leaned against the trunk of a large tree, closing her eyes momentarily before answering, "You're pregnant."

I nodded. "I think so."

"How long?"

"I haven't had a period since June."

Her chapped hands flew to her face. "Oh dear, oh dear."

"I'm sorry."

Her hand clenched the branch as she ripped off several leaves, crushing them in her palm. "You should have told me before school started. It would've been easier to hide." Then sheer terror filled her eyes, a terror I understood too well.

"Oh my God," her flushed face suddenly paled, "how will we tell your father?"

"Do we have to?" I had counted on her to figure out a way to hide it from him. She was good at that sort of thing.

"Let's make sure first," she replied.

Relief swept over my body in waves. Perhaps I was wrong. How stupid I was to even tell my mother. I should have found out myself before I told anyone.

A FEW DAYS later, the pregnancy results were confirmed. Mom had taken me to our local doctor. I was horrified that he

would know and wanted to go somewhere far away but she assured me that he wasn't allowed to tell anyone. "If the results are positive, I promise I'll arrange a doctor and hospital where no one knows you."

Now standing in the kitchen, Mom insisted we give my father the news. I thought I would vomit for the third time that day as I watched her pour him a drink. Her hands were shaking and she didn't water the rum down as she usually did. Then she poured a second glass for herself.

Pausing for a moment, she studied me and said, "What the hell," and filled a small glass with lots of Coke then topped it with a splash of rum and handed it to me. She signaled for me to follow her to the living room where my father waited. His stern face indicated that he knew the news wasn't good.

I reached for his package of Export A's on the side table and took out a cigarette. He automatically struck a match and held it to me as I leaned over. My hands trembling as I puffed until the cigarette took. It tasted of charcoal and I felt the harshness down my throat, holding it in for a moment before exhaling simultaneously through my mouth and nose.

Sunlight poured through the bay window lighting dust particles floating in the air. Outside the maples were just beginning to turn scarlet. I put my arms around Jeff and carried him to sit in the sun. He was only three. My father cut his hair as he had mine when I was young. The straight blonde hair looked as though he had placed a bowl upside down to measure where to

cut. The poor kid looked like one of the Three Stooges. He wanted to play paddy cake and kept trying to lift my hands in the air to clap. I watched my mother sitting at the opposite end of our rose colored couch as she spoke quietly, her hands folded on her lap. I couldn't hear her words with my brother happily repeating, 'paddy cake, paddy cake'. Jeff's entire body jerked when Dad bellowed, "I warned you this would happen."

Mom's head collapsed and her mouth tightened as she fidgeted with her ring. I hated how Dad blamed her for everything.

I squeezed my brother tight as he burrowed into my shoulder and placed his hands over his ears.

My mother was forty-eight, old for being the mother of a three year old. I had been thirteen when my younger brother was born. At first, Mom thought she was going through menopause and was horrified to discover she was pregnant. She was a big woman and hid her pregnancy with heavy winter coats when she went outdoors, but inside she couldn't hide from me. She simply chose not to discuss it until she was eight months along. As though I wouldn't know. Doug was away at Royal Roads Military College and had no idea Mom was expecting. I did write to warn him before he came home for Christmas.

I thought I'd die of embarrassment when everyone discovered that my parents still did 'it', but the first time I saw my brother's face, I fell in love. Forever.

Mom's hair was still blonde thanks to chemicals, but her waist was spreading and her lips drooped with the same sadness that often filled her eyes.

Dad had always been frightening –a tall, thin, stern man. Now at 59, his back slumped and his weary eyes held an enraged expression expecting the worse. He looked worn down. Both their spirits appeared broken as my parents discussed the latest in a lifetime of upsets.

I focused on the oil painting behind him, remembering the story my father always told about how Winston Churchill had come up behind him and complimented his style. 'I was influenced by the Group of Seven when I cooked for them on weekend outings during school,' he told the Prime Minister. And me - a thousand times.

My father was always telling stories. Like how he won the money to go to art school by placing his one and only bet ever on a horse. He had been fiddling with his pen and when the penclip fell off and hit the name of a horse called Penclip in the newspaper. He'd called a bookie. He told him to place a $15 bet 'across the board' meaning $5 to win, $5 to place and $5 to show. The bookie understood $15 for each spot. When the horse came in, Dad claimed he won a small fortune. Or when he met Walt Disney while painting movies sets in Hollywood. I used to believe his bullshit.

I wanted to take Jeff out of the room but didn't dare move. Even though my parents barely acknowledged our

presence, I knew if I stood to leave, Dad would turn his anger on us so I sat quietly praying my brother didn't understand.

Suddenly his tirade stopped. Turning towards me, he announced, "She'll get an abortion."

Mom gasped, "What about that girl up the street who died?" That was the first I'd heard of it. So I wasn't the only bad girl in town.

Mom responded firmly, "I can't allow some stranger to shove a spoke into my little girl's uterus." My body shuddered along with hers at the graphic image.

My father stopped pacing, "We'll send her to England. It's legal there."

Mom pulled back slightly, "We can't afford it."

"Borrow the money from one of your sisters."

Mom looked truly horrified at this suggestion. Her knuckles whitened as she gripped the arms of her chair, "God, no." For her, there was never any thought of sending me to one of her wealthy siblings or asking for help. "They are not to be told."

I agreed. Too ashamed, I would rather go into hiding than live in luxury if it meant they found out.

I saw my father's face crumble inward as he gave me a sad glance then dropped his face into his hands. I think I heard him mutter, "I'm sorry I've failed you."

EVENTUALLY, IT WAS decided to send me to an aunt and sick uncle I barely knew. I quit grade ten the following week under the guise of taking care of him.

We rarely visited my father's relatives. Dad had run away from home when he was fifteen, lied about his age, and joined the navy. He had rarely spoken to his family since. His brother lived in the poorest of the blue-collar neighbourhoods in Hamilton where rows of run-down housing projects owned by the Steel Company of Canada, lined a busy street in the industrial area of town. It reminded me of the slums around Jarvis and Parliament in Toronto where my mother closed the car windows, locked the doors and drove faster if we had to pass through. I never thought about how poor those people were until my father stopped in front of my uncle's house and I realized where I was going to have to live for the next several months. The homes were built right up to the sidewalk and kids played field hockey across the street on a concrete parking lot. My aunt had attempted to improve the place by painting the exterior a cheery pink and she nurtured a small patch of garden between the front door and the cement sidewalk although the flowers were brown and wilted in the autumn sun.

I shared a cramped room with my new-found cousin. She was in her thirties, never married, and worked in a hospital cafeteria. A bit plumpish, she was cheerful and seemed genuinely excited about having me there. My uncle was pale and coughed endlessly. He wasn't so pleased and seemed to resent the attention his wife and daughter lavished on me. I tried to stay out of his way when he came home from work but he sent me back to my parents after a few weeks.

My parents discussed other options, such as a home for unwed mothers, but money was always an issue so they decided I would spend the duration of my pregnancy hidden in our basement.

It's difficult to imagine this happened to me. It couldn't be me. But it was. So for the last five months of my pregnancy, I hid in that basement room. My mother died there several years later and part of me died the winter I was held captive within it's walls.

CHAPTER 3

OURS WAS A post-WWII home in a Toronto suburb bordering on the Rouge Valley. Like us, the neighbours were ordinary middle class people. None of my friend's parents were wealthy, so no one felt deprived. Except me. I had my mother's rich relatives for comparison.

The houses were box shaped set on deep lots, which were reminiscent of previous rural days. When Dad came home from the war, he purchased the land with a veteran's loan and some help from my mother's family. Ours was an open field with a poorly constructed brick house dropped in the middle. The previous owner had actually given it a name, Nymphfield Cottage, conjuring up images of naked ladies engaged in orgies which was a far cry from the reality.

Dad converted the field, working diligently to remove the weeds and tall grass and convert it into lawns and gardens. He planted grapevines to make his own wine. Cherry, plum, pear and peach trees, laden with fruit, were sprinkled around the grounds. His garden held every flower imaginable: tulips, daisies, gladiolas, pansies, mums, all bursting with color. Forsythia bushes, which lined one border were the first to burst out each spring in a flurry of yellow. Poplar trees lined the south edge. I loved the murmur of the leaves rustling in the breeze, a slow lingering sound not unlike a lazy creek washing over pebbles.

The sweet fragrance of lilacs perfumed each spring. There was even a small patch of bamboo where the driveway made its first turn. There's something lush and exotic about bamboo. The sway of the leaves, in summer, whispered to me as a child. Only my father's garden had it. Amazingly, the tropical foliage survived fierce Ontario winters.

A big old crabapple tree stood proudly close to the bamboo. It was the best to climb. All the kids loved that tree. Mom photographed it, an umbrella of white blossoms each spring and then branches weighed down by tiny red apples to be picked for jelly each fall.

Behind the garage, Dad left a few acres as field where a neighbour paid to board his two horses. Mom and I would pick wild asparagus there every spring.

On one side of the field, was a large hole where my older brother had once tried to dig his way to China. Someone had dragged a musty old mattress there and covered the top with boards and sticks to make a hidden fort. All the kids in the neighbourhood hung out there at one time or another. A teenager started a fire one summer when she was sneaking a cigarette. The smell of smoke alerted my mother who phoned the fire department. I remember the excitement of the firemen dousing the flames which spread quickly through the tall grass.

Despite the grueling hours Dad put in transforming the yard, the house remained the same square red brick bungalow. With only two bedrooms, one of us kids were forced to sleep in the basement. My brothers and I all used it as our bedroom as

soon as the previous sibling left home. Until my secret tenure began, the room in our basement had represented refuge from my parents. It was a large room, about fourteen by twenty feet and intended for use as a recreation room, not as a bedroom and certainly not a prison.

The ceiling was low with exposed pipes where the plaster had fallen away. The first floor toilet overflowed once and the hole was never repaired, but despite the ugliness, we kids willingly moved in just the same. I painted the walls burgundy when my turn came after Doug left for university. There was a desk in the corner, which I had painted pink and then covered the writing surface with beer labels I had collected by writing to various breweries. I covered it with a sheet of glass. A ragged, well-loved doll sat on the old couch, which stood in one corner.

My pride was the floor lamp beside my bed, which Mom had let me pick out. We had driven to an old barn, which had been converted into a furniture store. The ad declared the prices were lower than in town because the owners didn't need to pay rent. They removed the cows and shoveled out the dung filled straw and filled it to the brim with furniture. I chose a floor lamp with two brass poles of different heights topped with mauve shades. It felt like an extravagant gift at the time.

Outside the bedroom door, Dad's homemade wine fermented in vats and in winter, Mom hung wet laundry to dry near the laundry sinks when it was too cold to use the outside

clothesline. My brothers and I hung our clothes to dry on a ceiling pipe in the adjacent storage room to avoid absorbing the fruity smell of Dad's dandelion wine or the damp musty smell of wet laundry.

The windows were located high up the wall at ground level. There were metal radiators underneath which I used to stand on so that I could crawl through the windows late at night after my parents had gone to bed. I snuck out often during the summer of 1965 to meet the boy who got me pregnant. Later, those windows became my only source of daylight while I hid from the world and I grew up faster than I should have.

Directly above me was the bed on which my brothers and I were conceived. At night, I would lay in bed listening to my parents fighting, about Dad's drinking, but mostly about money. He would yell at my mother, defending his need to be self-employed as a printer. She begged him to get a nine to five job or else she'd be forced to borrow more money from her mother to pay our bills. "For Christ's sake, Elaine, I'll take care of my own family. I don't want you running home to mommy with your hand out every time I have a bad month." She'd yell back, "If you collected all your bills and stopped letting customers off the hook, I wouldn't have to" My father never turned down any work. Often a new restaurant couldn't pay for printing menus or business cards so we'd get a credit instead. Mom hated us eating out instead of getting paid. "The money goes so much further

buying groceries." But I loved being able to take my friends to the local pizza or Chinese joint to use up the money owed to Scarborough Litho. When Dad did get paid for a big printing job, he went on a spending spree, blowing it on dinners out and taking us shopping at Reitman's where he loved to pick out new dresses in colorful patterns for Mom and I.

But during that winter, the arguments were about my situation, each blaming the other for my predicament.

CHAPTER 4

WE LOOKED THE same – monochromatic. I like that word. It makes me think of my brothers and me with our hazel eyes and straight blonde, haystack hair, oval faces and crooked smiles angled like the Tower of Pisa. We had similar happy natures and when we laughed, we would begin and end at precisely the same moment. Mom and Dad were reflected in our faces, but I sometimes thought of my family as only my brothers and myself. With twenty years between the boys, I would pretend Doug was my husband and Jeff, our baby.

Doug reserved movie premières for me, mostly musicals - Oklahoma, South Pacific and the last one, we went to see was The Sound of Music at the Tivoli theatre in downtown Toronto with its gigantic chandeliers above the lobby and a 'Gone With The Wind' winding staircase leading to the balcony. I held my brother's arm, proud to be his date. Opening night was a huge event with advanced tickets sales only and everyone dressed up. We quickly memorized the lyrics and sang them together at the top of lungs while doing dishes or driving.

Doug had been the first to move into the basement. It must have been when he was six, after I was born. Doug was ambitious and got a paper route when he was nine. He won a trip to New York City for signing up the most new customers for The Telegraph. In high school, he got straight A's and was

involved in the Debate Club, the yearbook, as well as being president of the Camera Club. He became so skilled at photography that he gave up his paper route and concentrated on establishing a successful portrait business, buying camera and developing equipment with the money he had saved. He even built a studio downstairs.

He won a prize with a photo he took of me. He insisted I wear a plain blouse and plaid pants, which I felt was too drab and not the image I had in mind. I wanted to be glamorous like the models in the fashion magazines but instead I looked virginal. Then he made me pretend to play the accordion. The accordion! If I ever took up an instrument, it would be the drums or the guitar, never an accordion. Even though he won first prize, I never showed any of my friends the picture of me looking so weird. It must have been the image Doug wanted to create - a clean-cut, well-adjusted teenager from a Father Knows Best type of family. I suspect he couldn't cope with the real sister developing in front of him.

As a teenager, he had saved enough money to start investing in the stock market under the tutelage of our Uncle Basil. His first trade was a camera chain taken over by Black's Camera which still trades on the stock exchange today. He made a big profit, part of which he splurged on an extravagant restaurant dinner for the whole family. Mom made a fuss

about 'Dougie picking up the bill.' I was so proud of my big brother.

He won several university scholarships and chose to attend Royal Roads Military College three thousand miles away in British Columbia. I suspected he wanted to move as far away as from my parents as possible.

When Doug arrived home from university for the holidays, he would wake me in the morning playing his gentle rendition of *Moon River* on the piano or would sneak next to my bed while I was sleeping and slip candy cinnamon hearts in my mouth until I woke up. He'd tussle my hair, "Time to get up sleepy head."

"Doug," I would yelp and leap into his arms as his deep-throated laughter would build momentum and fill the room. It was impossible not to laugh when Doug was around.

I adored my older brother and could never allow him to find out about my pregnancy.

I HEARD MY mother's footsteps on the stairs.

"Kit Kat or Coffee Crisp?" She held out her daily offering as though chocolate could make my life sweeter.

I sat up on the bed and grabbed both candy bars. "When is Doug coming home?"

"Sometime around December 20th, Dear," she answered twisting the corners of her apron in her hands. She never looked directly at me the entire time I was pregnant.

"Can't I go back to Hamilton? To Uncle Jack's just for the holidays?"

"You know your uncle isn't well enough."

"I don't want Doug to find out." I swung my feet on to the floor and leaned forward. "Please don't tell him."

"How are we supposed to hide it?" She clenched and unclenched her hands. "Please, please don't tell him." She wouldn't look at me. I grabbed her skirt. "I'll die if he finds out."

She patted me on the head, and with a long sigh said, "You'll be seven months by Christmas." She glanced at my stomach. "You're already huge."

"I'll go anywhere. Surely there's some place?" I felt my throat constrict and my heart tightened as it did every time I thought about my brother discovering who his little sister really was.

"We'll see. Perhaps there's some way to work it out."

Doug stayed with his girlfriend's family that Christmas. He didn't visit us and flew back to school right after the New Year. I assumed that my mother told him. I never asked. I was simply relieved I didn't need to face him.

CHAPTER 5

BORED. I WAS so bored. No one to talk to. Nothing to do. I couldn't discuss my real feelings with my mother. It was my younger brother who kept me from going crazy. Jeff turned three during the winter of my imprisonment and he was the only one I could confide in and who appeared to love me no matter what. When he was older, he remembered nothing of my disgrace. I worried that he heard distorted rumors, especially the one told years later that he was not my parent's son, but mine. But I'm certain he never had an inkling. When it was over, no one in the family ever discussed those days or my baby again.

My world revolved around my little brother that winter. We played Simon says, or clapped patty cake and if his favorite song, 'Downtown' came on the radio, it was a moment of pure joy as we danced to the music. He would holler out the only word he knew, 'downtown'. Sometimes, he would hold our tabby cat, Licorice, by the belly as he danced. She endured being dragged across the room and never scratched him. At the end of the song, we would collapse in laughter and kisses.

My theme song that winter was, Eric Heatherly's hit,

about smoking cigarettes and counting flowers on the wall.

Of course I smoked. Everyone did. If you didn't, the kids at school pretty much pressured you to start. I began at age fourteen when a girlfriend moved downtown and invited me for the weekend. She told me that we were going to a party and she'd die of embarrassment unless I smoked. So we hid in the park across from her parent's house where I puffed on an Export A's, coughing on the harsh charcoal flavor burning my throat until she taught me how to inhale the smoke deep into my lungs. She'd proudly demonstrate how she could exhale through her nose or blow smoke rings or even using her tongue and teeth to flip the lit cigarette inside her mouth and close her lips to hide it. All of which I eventually learned how to do.

I didn't quit when I got pregnant. No one thought anything of it and cigarettes helped stem the boredom. But if Jeff tried to touch my cigarette package or an ashtray, I would scold him, "Bad, bad." Every time I lit up, I became "bad", only he couldn't quite pronounce bad so I became "Bab," a nickname which stuck for life.

In the afternoons, I'd curl up with him and read, pointing to the pictures in his books. He would gaze at me, fascinated by

the stories and I could see my reflection in his wide eyes. He would hold onto part of the book with his chubby little hands and repeat the words, “dog, cat, “or sound various animal noises until his hazel eyes started to close. He would struggle to stay awake, forcing his eyes open again, only to have them droop shut. His head would jerk until sleep overtook him.

I would stare at his innocent face while he slept, observing how his long blonde eyelashes fluttered as he dreamed, wondering what thoughts filled his young mind. I’d brush wisps of blonde hair behind his ears or gently stroking his soft skin while devouring the chocolate bars my mother brought me each day.

Every afternoon, I would listen as my classmates walked home from school together. I could hear their laughter and when the loneliness overpowered me, it was Jeff who hugged my tears away. Too young to judge, he became my only ally.

MY FRIENDS WROTE letters and my uncle forwarded them to me. I answered, mailing my letters back to my uncle to be re-sent from Hamilton. I wrote bullshit about my uncle’s health, my aunt and cousins and how much fun I was having with them.

I developed an anxious lethargy. If there could be such a combination of terms. If I was upstairs with my parents, I was constantly aware of any outside noises which left me poised to flee into the basement if someone unexpectedly visited.

Several of my friends visited my parents over the winter. They would ask how I was doing, while I remained hidden, listening to their conversations and struggling not to make any noise.

When people visited, Jeff never gave away my secret. One time, he called for me but Mom whisked him into his room and explained to the visitor how he missed me terribly now that I was 'away in Hamilton'. Somehow, he seemed to understand the necessity for secrecy because he never mentioned my name in front of visitors again. Usually, we were together in the basement so Mom would simply tell callers he was taking a nap.

One afternoon, a classmate, Linda, visited. Jeff and I were sitting in the living room watching Captain Kangaroo on television. As soon as I heard her knock on the door, I ran as fast as my bulky body would allow. I had gained so much weight, fifty pounds at least. Mom held her finger to her lips and waited to open the door until I escaped downstairs.

I could hear their voices clearly from my hideaway. Linda quizzed my parents about my sick uncle. She fired question after question at them.

"Is her uncle very ill?"

I could picture Mom in her chair, visibly upset. "Yes, Margie's Uncle Jack is extremely sick. It's unlikely she'll leave any time soon."

"Will she come home for Christmas?"

"We'll have to wait and see."

"Can I visit her in Hamilton one weekend?" Linda persisted in her interrogation.

"Walter's brother lives in a small house. There isn't a room for you to sleep in" Mom hated to lie and would do anything to avoid it.

While growing up, if I, for some reason, refused to talk to someone on the phone, my mother would insist I stand in an empty bathtub. Then she could honestly say, "Margie's in the bath right now. Can I take a message?" She justified that it wasn't really a lie because I was, after all, standing in the bathtub. Or she would make me go outdoors so she could tell the caller I was out and she didn't know *exactly* where I was at the moment.

With Linda sitting across from her and me hidden below, it must have been hell for my mother. Dad never liked Linda, so he sat on the couch, drink in hand, buried behind the newspaper. Ignoring the situation completely, he forced Mom to do the lying.

After I had given birth and supposedly returned home from taking care of my sick uncle, Linda boldly handed me a greeting card, which read, "I hear you had a baby. Why don't you get married next time?" The bitch. She was the only person who actually mentioned my pregnancy to my face. I never admitted it to her. I wouldn't give her the satisfaction. It was as though my predicament somehow made her feel the better person. Years later, I heard she married a man even though she had caught him in bed with another guy. She thought she could change him, certain he would give up his sexual preference after they were married. He didn't. They had a child and Linda willingly gave up her baby to be raised by her parents when her marriage fell apart. But the day she visited my parents during the winter of 1966, neither of us knew the future so she felt superior and I hated her for it.

WHEN MY FATHER started bringing me work from his printing shop, I leapt at the chance to do something useful.

In 1966, my father's small business couldn't afford any sophisticated equipment. Most jobs were labor intensive. My older brother and I had grown up helping. Often, the entire family would work together in the evenings while watching Bonanza or Ed Sullivan. We weren't paid. We were expected to

help out but if Dad needed kids from the neighbourhood to assist in a big job, he paid them .25 cents/hour and then and only then, would he pay us equally.

Collating was the most routine job. The family would form a small parade in the living room, moving along numbered pages, putting them together into a small booklet for one of Dad's customers. With my incarceration, he now had free, fulltime help.

I lined up piles of freshly lithographed papers, taking one from each pile, moving along the fireplace mantel to the arm – seat – arm of my mother's chair, picking up the pages lined along the piano bench, across the dining room table bundles to the piles along the couch.

When completed, I would tap the pages into a tidy package and place it crisscross on top of the previous one so my father was able to take one at a time and staple, glue or otherwise bind each completed set which might comprise ten to one hundred pages.

This chore involved a mindless rhythm that carried me away and allowed my mind to dwell on happier times when I wasn't glancing out the window to ensure no one could see me

from the road. Fortunately, the house was set back behind a large hedge so during the day it was difficult to see in with no lights on.

Vercatyping required more concentration. This process was used to raise the printed type on business cards. It was an expensive process which was supposed to imply success by the owner of such a card and impress the recipient. I doubt anyone consciously realized the words on the card were raised but holding each finished product in my hand, I marveled at how nice this added touch improved the appearance.

I would plug in a single electric hot plate or electric element and dip the card in a white powder, then hold it with tweezers over the heat while it did it's magic. The trick was to make sure I didn't hold it too close to the heater which would leave a smokymark on the back or so close I burnt my fingers.

These chores helped me escape the time and boredom.

CHAPTER 6

I KNEW WHAT they wanted me to say. All of them, but I couldn't.

I shifted uncomfortably in the hard chair, across from the social worker at Children's Aid. It was a sterile government office with white walls turned a faded gray. The agency was responsible for counseling unwed mothers, interviewing the fathers, as well as both sets of grandparents and then matching newborns with adoptive families.

I ran my hands along the edge of my chair and a splinter dug into my finger from the chipped wood. My mother sat next to me and watched as I sucked at the salty blood and tried to bite out the splinter. Dad never came with us. He could barely look at me now. As my tummy grew bigger, he avoided me as much as he could, never coming into the basement to see how I was doing.

The social worker sat behind a gray metal desk where she announced, "The boy has offered to marry you."

There was no romantic proposal in the moonlight. I hadn't seen Mark in months. When I first told him I was pregnant, he claimed the baby wasn't his. Now he wanted to

marry me. I imagined him being dragged to the office by his family.

My mother wanted me to accept. She looked genuinely relieved. So did the social worker. Marriage would make it all legitimate. They wanted to believe I was having Mark's baby because I loved him. It simply wasn't true and now I had to admit that secret along with all the other shameful feelings. Head held low over my chest, I mumbled, "I don't want to."

"Could you speak up please, Dear." the social worker asked.

"I don't want to marry him," I repeated louder.

"Margie, he's doing the right thing." My mother sounded exasperated. "Surely you want to marry him?"

"I don't want to." I shot an angry look at her.

Her face searched mine for the answer she so dearly needed to hear. "Of course you'll marry the boy."

"No, Mom, I won't." This time I looked her in the eye.

Mom slumped, then started to say something. The social worker interrupted, "Can I have a moment alone with your daughter?"

"Of course." My mother stood. She looked so bewildered, twisting her hands and standing with a defeated hunch to her shoulders. She stared at me then glanced at the woman behind the desk with an expression that implied, 'please talk some sense into my daughter'.

The social worker nodded towards the exit so she turned and went into the lobby closing the door with a forcible bang.

"Are you certain you don't want to marry the boy, Dear?" The social worker asked. Her voice was soft, not accusing like my mother's. She had dark hair and a Mediterranean look. She took her thick glasses off and held them in her hand as she observed me intently. Her hair was pulled tight in a bun at the back of her head and she kept calling me 'Dear' but she wasn't much older than I was.

"No way. I'm not forcing anyone to marry me. Besides, I don't love him." I could feel the heat turning my face crimson. I felt so ashamed to admit that I'd been having sex with a boy I didn't love.

"Then you intend to give your baby up for adoption?"

"I don't have any choice, do I?"

"As far as this agency is concerned, you have the final say in what happens to your baby. Neither your parents nor the father can tell you what to do. I'm here to help you make the right decision."

She paused and looked into my eyes before continuing. "You could keep it of course, but your baby would be born out of wedlock. Socially, this would be difficult for both of you." Her kind eyes searched mine.

"I don't want to do that to my baby."

"What do you want?" she asked.

"I want to do what's right. You should understand my dilemma."

"Because I work in the adoption agency?"

"No, 'cos we're about the same age. Could you give up your baby or marry some guy you didn't love?"

"Hmm, I see," she murmured. "I'm actually quite a bit older."

"You don't look it."

"Well, I've finished my Masters degree in social work and have been doing this for two years now." She leaned across her desk and looked straight into my eyes, "I worry about playing God. Every time I place a baby with a new family, I pray that I've done the right thing." She placed her hands on mine and squeezed, "Help me."

"I want my baby to be happy."

"Of course you do." She smiled. "You seem like a mature girl. I know it's difficult talking in front of your mother. Let's find out a bit about you so I can make a match you would approve of."

"Okay."

"Tell me a bit about yourself. What do you like to do?"

"I like reading. And horses."

"Tell me what kind of home you would choose for your baby."

"I want it to be a religious family."

"Which faith?"

"I don't care. As long as they believe in God."

"You believe in God?"

"Oh yes. God is God. All religions are defining the same thing."

She wrote some notes on her pad and continued, "Will you go back to school?"

"I want to," I confessed, "but I don't think I can face them."

"Who?"

"Everyone. My girlfriends, the teachers, and all the catty people who will gossip about me."

"Do you really think your friends would be so mean?"

"I know they will. No one will say anything to my face, but they'll all talk behind my back."

"What will you do?"

"I've worked part time since I was thirteen. I'll find something."

"You're a smart girl. Surely you want an education?"

My shoulders slumped. Yes, I did want to keep studying, but how could I face anyone?

"The boy's parents have offered to help you with any expenses."

"I don't want anything from him."

"What about your parents? Wouldn't it help them out?"

"I guess. Talk to my mother. I don't want anything to do with him."

"You're absolutely certain you would rather give up your baby than marry this boy?"

My heart tightened when she put it this way. I paused to consider my choices but it was Paul I loved. I had only slept with Mark for revenge. I was never in love with him.

I HAD MET Paul one year earlier. He honked at my girlfriend and I when we were walking home from the mall. We waved at the handsome blonde with the top down on his baby blue Mustang so he slammed on the brakes and pulled over. We didn't hesitate to run up and hop in. I found out later that he called his car, 'Virgin Bait'. And it was. When his sparkling blue eyes beckoned, I thought of moonlit skies and necking in drive-in theatres. I wanted to be the girl in his back seat.

I played the 'no no' game as long as I could but it was just a matter of time. We went to the drive-in but never saw the movie. Paul spent the evening groping and I held him back as best I could. We'd take drives in the country with the top down on the Mustang. I loved the feel of the wind in my hair but inevitably we'd end up necking on the grass somewhere with Paul trying to shove his hand up my grass stained dress. Or he'd park in some remote place. He seemed to know every dead-ended country road. I constantly worried someone would drive by and see us. Yet each time I saw him, I allowed him to go a bit further but never all the way.

The night I 'gave in' was a rainy October night in 1964. We broke into the shell of a house being built in the neighbourhood. The rain hammered against the unfinished roof as we stretched out on top of some bags of cement. Paul tugged at my skirt, urgently shifting it out of his way. I tried to slow him down, but our adolescent desire had a life of its own. There was no way I could not respond, tasting his minty breath as he kissed me, hard and demanding, while one hand grasping my breasts and the other sliding into my underpants.

The month of saying no washed away like the rain pouring off the roof as he pushed down my panties. When he finally collapsed, I remained still and listened as his breath gradually began to slow. Ignoring the discomfort of being trapped between Paul's weight and the hard surface of the floor, I gently stroked his blonde curls and nuzzled his neck. Finally, he rolled off me. "That was good."

Torn between tears and smiling, I felt my youth had vanished yet I didn't feel grown up as I had expected. I desperately needed reassurance but couldn't ask. My sense of self worth was demeaned and I felt like shit, yet also somehow triumphant. As though I owned Paul. I was certain this so-called act of love-making would bind us together for all time.

I WAS WRONG. He saw me when he was horny. Any body would have sufficed. But more and more, I sat waiting for the phone to ring. When we did see each other, it was to make love. Well, fuck really. It didn't feel like love to me. He said he loved me, insisted he would still respect me, but he didn't.

We made out wherever we could - in the backseat of his car on deserted roads, hidden in the tall grass on sunny afternoons, trying to say no but wanting to say yes.

The bitter sweet sense of having him so close yet knowing it was wrong. Once, at the drive-in, we were caught with the usher's humiliating light revealing our awkward state of undress.

The hurried cover up. The shame. After, I refused to do it in public again, so Paul checked us into a cheap motel room while I slumped down in his car, hiding from the lecherous motel manager peering out the window.

For girls, staying a virgin until marriage and for boys, marrying a virgin was the proper thing to do in the Sixties even though most of us were experimenting with sex. So eventually, Paul let me know he intended to marry a virgin, something he conveniently forgot to mention when he was in hot pursuit.

Devastated, I wept for hours in my room. I remember my father getting angry. "Get in here for dinner," he would demand, night after night as though his commands could stop my grief.

My mother would softly knock at my door and ask to come in. She sat on my bed, stoking my hair, "I know you're upset, Dear, but there will be many more Pauls in your life before you're old enough to marry." I pulled the pillow tighter over my head, "God, I hope not."

ACTUALLY, I THINK I missed Paul's family more than Paul. I wanted his parents, not mine. I wanted his lifestyle more than I wanted him. I often went to his house after school to play cards with his mother. She was a little chubby, like my mom, and about the same height, but the comparison ended there. Her short hair was curly and a natural auburn. Her dresses were plain but you could tell the quality. She told me, "Better to have one good dress than a bunch of cheap-looking things." I think her comments

influenced my decision to get my first job and splurge on clothing. Flo always had time for me and we would talk for hours over tea and home baked goodies. My mother was always in a hurry or upset over something my father had done. To my mind, Flo was the perfect mother. She listened intently and never rushed me.

When my mother asked me why I liked Flo so much. I told her how Flo would wait at the door or window and wave goodbye until I was out of sight. From that moment on, Mom did the same thing, but somehow it wasn't the same. I realize now that Mom must have been jealous and wanted me to love her the same way I loved Paul's mother. I should have been nicer but back then I didn't respect my mother for staying with my father. For not providing me with the same lifestyle as Flo gave her family or for not marrying an affluent man the way her sisters had.

Paul worked for his dad after school, so they would come home together and his mom seemed to have dinner ready no matter how long I hung out there after school. Paul would get angry at me for coming over all the time while his father called me 'Moonface' and made me feel welcome. Paul's home seemed so calm compared to mine. His parents never fought as far as I observed and his mother didn't complain about money. They owned a summer cottage near Peterborough and took me there once. I woke up at four in the morning to go fishing with Paul and his brothers. We caught lake trout and Flo fried them with eggs for breakfast. The earthy smell of the wood burning stove mixed with hot butter and fresh fish made our mouths water and

remained a memorable meal even after years had passed. It felt like being at one of my aunt's summer homes.

After Paul and I broke up, it was months before I ventured out of the house. My reputation was ruined because, of course, Paul bragged about his conquest around school. The boys would strip me with their eyes when I passed in the hallways. I'd see Paul occasionally but we always ended up in bed and I hated myself for not being strong enough to refuse seeing him.

I didn't date anyone else until I met Mark the following spring. He went to a different high school so Paul didn't know him. I wanted Mark to make Paul jealous, but it wasn't jealousy I sparked, only ownership.

"Someone must be cutting in on my grass," Paul had said when I would no longer sleep with him.

Paul eventually married his virgin. It had been easy for her to keep her virginity intact because he told me years later that she hated sex. Deprived, he tried several times to get back with me over the next few years, and it gave me great pleasure to hear him admit he had made a mistake when he dropped me.

When Paul's father died suddenly of a heart attack the winter I was pregnant and couldn't go to his funeral, I was devastated. Paul and his mother were certain I would come home from Hamilton. I longed to honor his father's memory and be there for Flo but of course, I couldn't.

I MET MARK one night after my girlfriends and I got together to drink a Mickie of gin in the schoolyard. One of the

other girls smoked a joint. When she offered me a drag, I said, "No way."

Later, we went to Harvey's where the burgers were grilled fresh over charcoal. The restaurant had only a few tables by a takeout counter so the parking lot was where everyone hung out listening to transistor radios unless someone blasted music from their car – like the risky new hit by the Rolling Stones, "I *can't get no satisfaction"*. We girls would sing along, giggling over the lyrics.

"It's pregnant," I was certain, "trying to get some girl pregnant"

"No way." one of the girls argued. "They can't sing that on radio."

"It's trying to get some girl to show me." Someone else volunteered

We'd argue endlessly over the words.

Usually about ten or more of us would stand around in small groups smoking and trying to look cool and uninterested in the others but taking in every aspect of the scene.

Lots of my girlfriends ironed their hair, envying my straight blonde locks while I dreamed of soft curls like Pussy Galore in Goldfinger. Or Sandra Dee. I was often told I looked like her. I knew all the words to the theme song from her movie, Tammy. But I wasn't gifted with curls so every Friday I would go to the hairdresser who looped individual strands into a beehive, held rock hard with hairspray. I'd wrap toilet paper around my

head every night for a week to try to maintain my coiffure until my next appointment.

The previous year, I had spent the summer at Patricia Stevens Finishing School. I convinced my mother to let me spend a little of the thousand dollars my grandmother had left each of her numerous grandchildren in her will. I wanted to learn how to be more like my wealthy cousins. Since taking the classes, I knew I shouldn't cross my legs in public and practiced walking as though a book was balanced on my head. I tried to be as sophisticated looking as Sandra Dee.

My friends wore mostly ripped jeans and colorful tank tops but I loved pretty clothes and spent every cent I made working at the Roxy theatre candy counter, on the latest fashions. I even owned a silver paper dress with a sequin neckline similar to one I had seen in the fashion magazines. "Where are you planning to wear that?" my mother demanded when I brought it home. I only wore it once to a party because my social life didn't include many special occasions. Sometime I'd dress up just for fun and pretend I was hosting a party in one of my aunt's homes.

The year before I bought a fake white fur coat with a fluffy collar. My parents refused to spend that kind of money on anything so impractical so I lied about my age, saying I was 16 and got the job at the theatre. It took me from April until Halloween night to pay off the $51.49 price tag on lay away. I wore it cautiously and became furious if a car splashed me once I discovered it cost $8 to dry clean it. I loved that coat.

The day I met Mark, I was wearing a deep blue floral granny skirt with a multicolored shirt I had tied-dyed yellow and orange. Trying to act the part, I wore my array of protest buttons: Warning, Your Local Police are Armed & Dangerous!, Never Trust Anyone Over 30! or 'PEOPLE POWER.

Mark looked so sexy that night at Harvey's, leaning against the wall in his bell bottom pants and black tee shirt with an army jacket slung over his shoulder, like Elvis or James Dean. He was a draft dodger. He often told me over the next few months that he could never kill those poor yellow bastards in Vietnam.

The war in Vietnam was a distant problem in Canada. I didn't know anyone who was fighting but I wore my array of protest buttons proudly. I'd never heard of Haight Ashbury, love-ins or the counter revolution at that time but signaled the universal peace sign whenever it felt appropriate. Even if I was too afraid to try drugs, I was hip.

"Smoke?" He asked as he took the package out of his rolled up sleeve.

"Sure." I took a cigarette, and held his lit one against mine for a light.

"You new around here? I haven't seen you before."

"I'm hanging out with my girlfriend, Cheryl. She just moved here." I explained. "I go to West Hill Collegiate."

"How'd you get here? Drive?"

"No, bus. I get my license next month when I turn sixteen. You?"

"I don't have a car. I hope to get a job and buy one but I just moved in with my aunt and uncle. I'm from the States."

"For the summer?"

"I'm finishing high school here. But," his eyes caressed my body, "I might stay longer if I like it." I think he put his arm around me at that point and I didn't object.

I wouldn't let Mark touch me inappropriately that night but I didn't resist for long. I constantly wished Paul would drive by and go crazy with jealousy if he saw me with this handsome dark-haired boy who was nuzzling my neck.

I GREW UP a lot in the years following those rolls in the hay with my apostles, Paul and Mark. Life forced me to.

CHAPTER 7

I HATED TUESDAYS. That was the day I went to the clinic for unwed mothers. I couldn't go to the doctor who had delivered me and watched me grow up because our neighbours might be in his waiting room. Instead, I went to a clinic downtown. The visit would start with the humiliating process of sneaking into the car without being seen. Mom would drive as close to the back door as possible. She would make sure the coast was clear and I would creep, almost crawling along the ground from the house to the car and slouch down on the back seat. I stretched out with my head down so nosey neighbours didn't see me, especially Mrs. Littlewood. She stared out her window and knew everything that was going on and made a point that everyone else knew as well. I felt I would die if she saw me. I waited until we were several blocks from the house before I felt safe to sit up.

At least these visits gave me a reason to get out of my baggy nightshirt and wear the one maternity dress that Mom had bought me. It was floral. Big blue and pink flowers swirling everywhere with puffy sleeves and an elastic empire waistline under my swollen breasts. I looked even bigger than I was. I won't wear floral patterns to this day.

Mom generally would drop me off and visit one of her sisters – the aunts who supposedly didn't know why she came

to town each Tuesday. She despised sitting with the other unwed mothers in the Government clinic. But occasionally, she would, and then take me out afterwards for lunch. Our family rarely went to restaurants, so she considered it a special treat. I hated the way some people would look at my gigantic stomach and whisper to each other.

I would sit on the hard wooden bench under the florescent lights and wait my turn. It was overcrowded with girls just like me in various stages of pregnancy, some barely showing and others so big they waddled to their seats and groaned with difficulty getting up when the doctor came out and called their name. Every week I saw a different doctor.

This week the doctor who examined me barely lifted his eyes. His white lab coat hung loosely on his fingerlike frame. With my eyes fixed on the floor, I noticed brown Oxfords peeking out below his black pants. He reminded me of a crow. His voice was shrill and his gaunt face was framed by straight black strands of greasy hair. He lifted his face toward me momentarily and dark eyes pierced through me.

"How are you feeling?"

"My legs hurt." I replied.

He motioned for me to lay back on the stretcher and took hold of my leg, "Yes, they are swollen. How much weight have you gained?"

"Sixty –three pounds."

"Not surprising your legs bother you. Pretty common. Try and watch your diet."

I thought about the chocolate my mother administered each day and knew I wasn't willing to give up my only pleasure.

"Okay, let's take a look."

I leaned back submissively while yet another stranger prodded and poked. This doctor had long slender fingers, which seemed to reach deep inside me. His wrist was so thin, I could feel his loose watch hit against my buttocks while he examined me.

"Everything's coming along nicely but remember, easy on the desserts." He left the room without another glance in my direction.

The previous internal exam was by a doctor with bushy red hair, who reminded me of Bozo The Clown. He had doused himself in Old Spice after shave. His hands were huge with fat pudgy fingers and I felt my body automatically stiffen as I watched him pull rubber gloves over perfectly manicured nails. He kept telling me to relax. Sure. That week, my fingers clenched the side of the stretcher and a little pee dribbled between my legs as he spread them apart. I closed my eyes and prayed for the examination to be over quickly.

The staff at the clinic knew I would be giving my baby up for adoption. They never discussed my baby in anything but terms of "the delivery". I felt as though I was simply a repository making a baby for strangers. I wanted them to see me as a human being with feelings of her own. Perhaps it was

too painful to become attached to the endless array of girls who came through their doors.

When the examination finished, I dressed quickly and went into to the reception area I dug into my purse for a cigarette, inhaling deeply, then exhaling loudly as though I could smoke the indignation away while I waited for my mother while observing the other unwed mothers sitting on benches beside me. Most of the other girls in the clinic kept their eyes to the floor and avoided talking, just tilting their heads in recognition.

I was probably one of the younger ones. Only Christine looked older than twenty. I guessed her age to be in the early thirties. She arrived at the clinic close to the end of my term. A tough looking platinum blonde with long black roots, she said she gave up bleaching her hair when she went into hiding. She caught me staring at the enormous diamond ring on her left hand. She snorted a laugh, waving her hand out with her fingers outstretched and said, "Yes it's a beauty but unfortunately it came from my ex." I must have looked confused so she continued, "I left him."

She lowered her hand and twisted the loose fitting ring around and around. "His money wasn't enough to make it worth staying. We owned a circus."

"Oh." I was amazed. I don't know who I thought would own a circus but I couldn't imagine it would be a man and wife.

"We were on the road most of the year. I thought it was exciting when we first met but that wore off real quick when he

started beating me." She rolled up her sleeve to reveal a large scar that dug through her forearm. "He had a vicious temper. This scar reminds me of his skill with a knife."

"Why would he do such a thing?" I was shocked. No matter how angry my father became when he drank, I had never seen him hit my mother. It was unimaginable to me.

"He was insanely jealous and accused me of sleeping with one of the crew. I actually had wanted to but wouldn't dare. He would have killed us both."

I looked towards her stomach. She was in the early stages of her pregnancy.

"Don't worry, it's his baby. But he'll never know. I ran away."

"Are you giving your baby up for adoption then?"

"God no." she looked fondly at her widening waistline, "It's one thing to hit me but that monster will never hurt my baby 'cos I'll make sure he never knows."

"How will you manage? Financially, I mean?"

"Well first off, I'll sell this." She glanced at the ring. "I'll replace it with a plain gold band and tell everyone my husband died."

"But how long will the money last?"

"Long enough to get me started anyway. I've rented a bed sitting room but once the baby is born, I plan to move to a small town somewhere and get a job. I used to work as a cocktail waitress."

"But that only pays minimum wage."

"In the right bar, the tips are great and", she looked around cautiously, "we cocktail waitresses have a pact that we only declare a small portion. We hide the rest in a safety deposit box. Besides, I socked away a lot of money when I was married to that jerk and at the end, I stole his secret stash."

"You stole it. Won't he come after you for the money?"

"Oh he'll come looking for me alright. Already has. But he doesn't know about the money I skimmed. I did the bookkeeping and the circus is a big cash business. Makes it easy to sneak some off the top. I think all wives should have a separate bank account that their husbands don't know about. Otherwise they're totally dependent on their husband and are forced to stay no matter how rotten they are. Not me." She pointed her finger at me, "Remember that when you get married. Always keep your own get-away stash."

"I don't know if I'll ever get married. Not now."

She patted my hand and in a motherly tone added, "Yes you will. This will soon be all behind you and there will be someone special for you. "

"I'm not holding my breath for any Prince Charming."

"Despite that bastard, I still believe there are men out there who know how to treat a women. At least two. One for you and one for me."

Christine's optimism made me smile whenever I saw her.

Then there was Donna. The memory of her situation stayed with me. One week we found ourselves sitting beside each other for an hour, waiting. Her eyebrows needed plucking but

then none of the girls in the clinic seemed to care much about their appearance. Freckles covered her face and arms. Short auburn hair framed her delicate features. She was so tiny, not more than five foot one.

Why she confided in me, I don't know but after just the most casual conversation, "How far along are you?" "Did you get morning sickness?" non- committal stuff, she announced, "I was raped."

I didn't know how to respond. "That's awful." I touched her hand. My face must have shown the horror I felt.

"Yeah, by two boys in the neighbourhood."

"Wow" Things could be worse, I thought.

Even in pregnancy, she was tiny. Her stomach seemed to stick out in front. Moving from behind her, it would be a shock to see the bulge in her otherwise slim body. She would never be able to defend herself against one boy let alone two. "Did they go to jail?"

"I didn't press charges."

"Why not?

"What's the point? They always make it look like the girl wanted to be raped. If I went to court, it would only become public."

Instantly, I felt her words in my chest - the familiar tightness of angry frustration – the frustration which comes from not being in control of the events impacting your life.

I moved closer on the bench and placed my hand on her shoulder. "They should be punished for what they did to you."

She shrugged in defeat and gave me a look, which clearly revealed she thought I was naive. With a defiant look as though daring me to contradict her, she announced. "I'm keeping my baby."

"Why?" I was shocked.

Her face softened as she touched her stomach gently. "It's mine." I guessed her to be around eighteen. Her sad brown eyes, shiny with tears met mine, her voice pleaded for understanding. "Something that truly belongs to me."

God, having a rapist as your father, I thought, is about as bad as it could get. "What if one of them shows up and demands visiting rights?"

The softness in her face disappeared, replaced by a fiery rage as she barked her response. "They don't know I'm pregnant. And who knows which one is the father? "Besides, I'm never going back home."

"What about your parents?" I asked.

"They'll have to come to me."

"Do they want to see their grandchild under these circumstances?"

She shrugged, "I guess I'll find out the answer to that question, won't I?"

"What will you tell your baby about the father?" I was fascinated with her determination.

"My baby doesn't have a father." Her voice contained a force that would stop any child from asking more questions.

I didn't push the issue further but had to ask one more time, "And if one of the boys finds out and comes looking. What then?"

"I'll kill him." She replied simply.

I believed her and marveled at her strength, especially when I didn't have the nerve to keep my baby. I've thought of her often over the years and wondered how things turned out. Whether the father found out about his child and how others accepted her situation. She made me think about women who were raped during wars. They probably had no choice but to keep their baby. How would a Jewish girl feel towards a baby resulting from rape by a Nazi soldier? Or a black slave raising the bastard child of her master? Do mothers love their babies no matter who fathered them? Could I? Wouldn't they see the face of the enemy every time they looked at their child? Would the pain ever dissolve? How could a small community accept these children when my family couldn't even acknowledge my pregnancy?

CHAPTER 8

I'M NOT SURE when the transition occurred. Perhaps it was a gradual coming to consciousness, but at some point my baby became real. Closing my eyes, mesmerized by the movements in my tummy, I savored the dance of life being performed within me. I would forget my feelings of helplessness and become protective. In those quiet moments, I enjoyed my pregnancy and was content to remain that way forever. I even allowed myself to dream of a life together.

One morning, I stood beside my young brother's bed and watched him awaken. There was a faint smile on his lips and I wondered what he had been dreaming about. His little face was so perfect, so angelic and free from worries. Overwhelmed, tears wet my cheek. *He is so beautiful.* I touched his face, his wispy blonde hairs and understood the miracle of birth, forgetting he wasn't mine. I felt my own baby awakening with a gentle kick. I smiled and patted the massive bulk of my tummy. "Good morning."

Late that night, I climbed the stairs and sat by the living room window watching the snow fall. The flakes appeared like crystals simmering on the lawn in the moonlight. My baby was awake. Embracing my protruding belly, I stood, beginning a slow dance in the moonlight. Closing my eyes, I imagined my baby was already born.

We are in an autumn forest, bright oranges, reds and gold. Leaves whirl about us. The rich scent of decaying leaves fills the air. I hold my baby in a tender embrace – dancing to life. Jeff dances with us - each of my babies holding my hand, the wind and leaves whirling around us. I no longer consider the 'how' of it or worry about how realistic a life together would be - we simply float in a wonderland of possibilities, my babies secure in my love. A gentle wind blows the colors around us, merging, alive, flowing with life. There are no threats in our forest, no dangers, no one telling us what to do. There are no judgments, no parents, no harsh words, and no boredom - only a kaleidoscope of fantasy. There is neither beginning nor end to us, and our forest. We dance as the sunlight shimmers amongst the trees. Its warm beams flow straight towards my heart, down my arms and out through their little palms, connecting us. I am motherhood, as we dance our dance of freedom.

Opening my eyes, I decided at that moment to demand that my mother help me keep my baby. Somehow, I would make her understand. Or I'd run away and take Jeff with me. We would be a family. I would find our forest of possibility.

MOM WAS HORRIFIED. "Oh dear, we can't afford it."

"I'll work. I'll pay you room and board." I sat on my bed. She stood across from me, arms limp and holding her daily

offering of chocolate, now forgotten. I leaned forward as I pleaded my case.

"Sweetheart, I understand," she sat beside me. "But I'm not young anymore and your father is almost sixty. We don't know how we'll cope with your brother let alone another child."

"I'll take care of them. I do already with Jeff. You won't need to." Surely she could see into my heart. I was determined to make her understand.

"Then how could you work? Children are expensive."

My face fell. "The night shift. I'll work the nightshift so I can be with them during the day."

"Don't be silly," she continued. "Your Dad and I thought we'd finally be able to have some time on our own with Doug gone and you growing up and think about retirement, but Jeff changed all that. We are thrilled to have him, but I simply can't manage two babies." She stood indicating the conversation was over.

I grabbed her hand, "Please, Mom. I'll do anything."

She looked at my hand and clasped it with both of hers. "It's better this way."

"Better for you!" I shook her away. She gasped, her face etched in pain, but I felt more sympathy for myself. Had my parents ever danced in a forest of possibility, where they just did what they needed to do without consideration? If so, they'd obviously forgotten years ago.

THEY MET AT a mutual friend's wedding. Dad, an usher, escorted my mother to her seat. He held her arm extra tight and whispered, "Such a beautie. Save me a dance, the first and the last." He had flirted outrageously, an unknown behavior in her conservative world. She was terribly shy and kept her eyes to the floor while she blushed a deep red.

She was being courted at the time by Philip, the boy who lived down the street. In her old photo album there was a picture of her standing beside him. It was the face of a woman who felt treasured. A full smile spread across her moon-shaped face. Her stylish blonde hairdo and expensive dress indicated privilege.

As a child, especially when Dad was drunk, I used to wonder what life would have been like for us, if she had married Philip instead of my father. Would I have been born? Of course not.

I would look at the photo of her smiling, Philip's hand in hers, in front of 191 as we called my grandparents' mansion where she grew up. Then, I would glance at her sitting by the fire in her chair which needed recovering as she mended old socks, the corners of her mouth turned down. You could see from the photographs, the shape of her mouth had changed direction over the years that followed.

My father's attraction as a starving artist combined with her rebellion as a spoiled child became her nemesis in life. After years of marriage, his sarcastic wit eroded her confidence and

obliterated her joie de vivre. It's no wonder, as a young girl, I longed for Philip and 191.

One magical night, Mom talked, really talked, about her past. Dad was out drinking and the house was quiet for a change. She put one of the Reader's Digest collection of classical music on the record player. It was Chopin, her favourite. I snuggled into her on the couch as she reminisced about her youth. She told me that she had been instantly enamored with my dad, a charming stranger in uniform. Six feet tall, slim, his blonde hair slicked back, a matching mustache under his laughing hazel eyes; he was dangerously older, with a worldliness and charm she had not experienced before.

"He was a handsome fellow, your father." She had said dreamily, "He seemed to swallow me up in those arms. I felt safe."

Then she laughed, "He held me so close on the dance floor, poor Philip stood by helplessly." I remembered how stiff her first love had looked in the old photographs. He was nice looking in a tailored sort of way. So different from my father, it's no wonder she was attracted to the naughty stranger.

"When Walter spoke about the war, the loneliness, his fear of dying in the trenches, I forgot Philip." I closed my eyes as she spoke and pictured my parents as a young couple dancing.

"His best friend was blown up right in front of him." Mom continued, "He felt guilty that he had only a little shrapnel in his thigh."

She seemed to forget I was there. "He winked and said he would show it to me sometime. The implication was clear and made me shiver from head to toe." She giggled, "The attraction was so physical, it transcended any apparent differences. I responded to him in a way I never felt with Philip. I imagined him a hero risking his life across Europe to personally save me from Hitler. I wanted to comfort him."

My mother brushed my hair away and kissed my forehead, "My parents loved Philip. He came from a good family. But I felt as though I could predict everything to my dying day if I married him. Whereas with your father, I wouldn't know what to expect. He told me that he hoped to work as a commercial artist when the war ended. Now, she confessed, the spark between them had died long ago. He had been her rebellion from a life of predictability, but the reality turned out differently. As a pampered girl, his Bohemian lifestyle appeared attractive but it was no longer fun to play in his world.

My father, the vibrant, eccentric artist became disillusioned over time with his wife and her family's expectations. He opened his own printing and commercial art company, funded by her family. It might have succeeded except for Hurricane Hazel in the 1950's, which destroyed everything and forced him to move the business into our garage. After that disaster, he started drinking and depression destroyed his joyful spirit. I guess in some ways she was too strong for him and destroyed the very spirit she fell in love with by setting a standard he could not live up to. Her judgment pushed him further into

despair and my mother became overwhelmed by the very change in his character.

I suppose that both of my parents let each other down. The passion disappeared along with their uniqueness – Dad's versatile strength and Mom's gentle shyness.

They made me glad I didn't marry the father of my baby.

CHAPTER 9

"OKAY, THEY TURNED out the lights." Mom moved away from the window and motioned me with a nod towards the back door.

"Not tonight, Mom. It's cold." I pulled the blanket tighter around my corpulent body and turned back to watch Get Smart on television.

"You must get some fresh air. It's not healthy being indoors all day long."

I groaned as I did every night when she pulled me by the arm and forced me to get up, slip on my father's winter coat and stand outdoors. We always waited until the last of the neighbours went to bed, usually around eleven each evening. On the nights the people next door stayed up for the news, I couldn't go out until midnight.

Sometimes my mother would bundle up and come out with me, holding her finger to her lips if I tried to speak but mostly she stood by the door and gave me the same warning every night, "Don't catch a cold. It's bad for the baby."

I would hold on tight to the banister as I made my way down the stairs and out the side door. I walked cautiously hugging the house. Each step crunched loudly on the icy sidewalk

and I prayed to stay hidden until I reached the enclosed garden behind the house. It was a secluded part of the yard I'd helped my father create years before. He wanted one place private from 'Nosey Parkers' referring to some of our neighbours. I appreciated his sentiment that winter more than ever. The garden was a sanctuary hidden by the house on one side, hedges to the east and north and the garage blocked the view of most of the south side. Dad had added a lattice fence with climbing rose bushes to close in the rest of the area.

My father had also built a pond there when I was four. I proudly helped scoop out the dirt with my toy shovel as he dug the hole. I remember the rich earthy smell of the freshly tossed dirt that my father used to build the lush garden beside the pond. After he poured the concrete, I squealed with fear and delight as he held me suspended over the wet cement and told me to make a palm print in the gooey surface. After he set me down, he leaned in and put his own print beside mine and whispered that it would be our secret mark of ownership. Once it dried, I watched excitedly, jumping up and down, clapping my hands as he filled it with water. At first we stocked it with goldfish, but the raccoons ate them in a few days so we settled for water lilies which flourished each summer. Mom and Dad would sit in lawn chairs beside the pond after work, hidden from the world and sip cocktails. Sometimes, they made me a Shirley Temple with maraschino cherry and a paper umbrella floating on the surface.

Now, on those winter nights, the pond was frozen solid. The snow blew in drifts so I leaned my back against the house

to avoid the wind and concentrated on taking in as much fresh air as possible then exhaled the frosty breath. Aluminum pie plates dangled from the Bing cherry tree and rattled endlessly in the wind. Dad and I tied them to the branches each year to ward off birds from devouring the fruit. Now the branches, weighted down from the heavy snowfall, were at risk of breaking.

Shifting from one foot to another, I could feel my baby kick in protest of the cold weather so I hugged my father's wool coat around my bulky frame. I wore a Russian style fur hat with the flaps pulled down to protect my ears. It was the hat_my brother, Doug, wore during the winter he parked cars at Club Killarnee, the fancy dinner place close by. When he arrived home after work, I would beg him to take his hat off because he always hid some treat for me under it- French fries or a dessert. The memory still makes me smile.

I would grow bored just standing around, so voluntarily returned to my prison. Even murderers got more time in the yard than I did that winter.

It was shortly after eleven one February night, when I came in from the cold and everyone was sleeping, that my water broke.

CHAPTER 10

LEGALLY I WAS required to name my baby. I called her Noel Markette. Noel, after the singer, Andy Williams, daughter. I'm not sure why I chose Markette because her father never expressed any interest in his child.

I considered running away with my baby, but what could I offer her?

The previous summer I had met a girl in Yorkville, who told me I could hang out at her place. She rented a large room in an old house on Huron Street. Everything, the carpets, the wallpaper, the furniture were ancient and smelled dusty and moldy.

She shared a bathroom down the hall. The male tenants never cleaned up their black hairs in the sink or tub and there were wet urine spots on the side of the toilet and on the floor. It grossed me out.

Her kitchen consisted of a two element hot plate set on a small cupboard for storing dry food. A communal refrigerator sat in the hall outside, but she said she couldn't leave any food in it because it would be stolen. I think she survived on peanut butter and Ritz crackers, tins of baked beans and potato chips.

Her bed was in an alcove partitioned off the main room by a beaded multi-colored plastic curtain. Anti-establishment posters

hung on the wall and a macramé, containing a dead fern hung in the large curtain-less bay window. She had a purple lava light, big pillows scattered everywhere and a bright orange beanbag chair.

She told me she left home because her parents were capitalist pigs. It seemed to me that some of that capital had paid for her big hi-fi and the stack of 33's.

An elaborate water pipe sat on the floor and she offered me some hashish. She wouldn't join me she said, because she had just dropped acid.

I left in a hurry.

I was certain that a boarding house downtown or some dark basement in the suburbs was not where I wanted my baby to grow up.

I GOT THE only job I could at sixteen, working in a factory on Spadina Road in the industrial area of Toronto. We made doll's eyeballs. The eye socket was placed in the machine with my right hand, the eyeball with the left, then the eyelid was set into ridges with my right hand while the left pulled down the lever. Heat melted the plastic, which sealed it all together. The burnt plastic smelled like incense gone bad. The monotony set in. The rhythm de-sensitized life. My only challenge was to beat yesterday's record, racing to increase the number of eyes per day. Thirteen hundred at the beginning now up to fifteen hundred until one of the other workers took me aside and demanded that I slow my production. 'We've worked here for years and can't work to your

pace. Once you've been here as long as we have, you won't work so hard either.'

Most of the women were war widows who found themselves raising their families alone when peace failed to bring their husbands home. I watched the old women sit in front of their machines turning out eyeballs to be fitted in some happy child's doll and I knew these women had died. Dead eyes sat in their sockets like the eyes they were making. I felt the women around me had given up.

At lunch I would sit alone in a small park across the street, refusing to hear more of their sad tales. It was my only escape from their reality, just as those late night breaths of fresh air beside the pond in our backyard had been my only escape on those nights I was pregnant. Mom was right. I didn't want to work in that factory for the rest of my life like those women.

DURING THE OBLIGATORY follow-up visit after my daughter's birth, the young social worker read me my rights. "You are allowed to visit your daughter at the foster mother's home for the first three months." In a forceful voice, she added, "However, I strongly advise against it. It will only make things more difficult for you, but I am required, by law, to advise you that you can."

Of course I went. I didn't tell anyone, certainly not my parents, and there was no one else to tell. I saw Noel several

times before I gave her up. Gave her up! Like she was some sort of an addiction that one wanted to get rid of.

Each week, I would sneak away and catch the bus to spend time with her. I sat in the living room of the foster family assigned to her care until an adoption became final, and watched her tiny face while the television showed how life continued, separate from us. Once, I saw the excited face of the winner of the Kentucky Derby. I knew what I would do if I won. Run away. But I didn't even know how to buy a ticket.

Noel was a happy baby, kicking her legs, squealing with laughter and very alert, taking in every movement. I enjoyed changing poop filled diapers and wiping her rosy bottom clean. Everything about her fascinated me. Her tiny fingers were so small yet held amazing strength when she grasped mine. It made me wonder if she knew I would soon leave her, but that was ridiculous.

I would rock her softly or feed her a bottle. When her little head banged against my chest, I felt my nipples instinctively leak milk. The damp bandages I wore were tight to cut off the flow of unused breast milk. I longed to breast feed my baby, to feel her against my nipple. What would it feel like, I wondered? I could feel a tug at my breast as though they also reached out for her touch. It was such a natural exchange between a mother and her child, but I was afraid. I wished I had the nerve to do it just once, but what if I got caught? The foster mother, Beatrice, might walk in on us. She reminded me of

Paul's mother, Flo, with her kind face and easy conversation. Bea never made me feel that I had done something disgraceful by having a baby out of wedlock but I doubted she would approved of me breast feeding, so I sat quietly on her couch, holding Noel, singing to her and dreaming of a life together. I held her head against my shoulder and rocked her while savoring her sweet baby smell, a mixture of talcum powder and that special sweet scent unique to newborns.

In May, on the last day I was allowed to visit, the foster mother said, "I have a camera. I'll take a picture of you with Noel, if you like."

"Oh, yes, please." I held her on the front porch overlooking noisy Warden Avenue with cars zipping by, honking. It was still cold but a bright sun was shining. Noel was dressed in a pink snowsuit, her tiny, oval face peaking out from underneath. Wisps of soft blonde curls escaped the hood. I held her up for the camera. So proud. She was perfect. Tiny fingers flayed against my mouth as frost escaped in the cool spring air. I grabbed her hands and sucked gently on her fingers, enjoying her sweet fruity taste.

"I'll mail copies to you after I get them developed." Bea promised.

She stood quietly and watched me snuggle Noel. Sadness emanated from her when she told me, "I applied to Children's Aid to adopt Noel."

I looked up with a start. I pulled Noel closer. Part of me was devastated by her news.

"I'm not allowed to adopt her." She continued.

"Oh? Why not?" I demanded. She was such a nice person and I could visit.

"You know me and aren't allowed to know where she lives."

"I'm not some criminal." I stammered.

"I know, Sweetie. But I guess they feel you would visit and never let go. The agency knows what's best for everyone involved."

My mouth felt parched.

"The social worker tells me that the people who are adopting her already have a little boy. He's two. They're very excited about getting a girl."

I couldn't speak. I felt sorry for the woman before me. She would have made a nice home for my Noel and I stood in her way.

Bea took me by the arm and led me indoors. The house felt hot after the crisp spring weather. Noel started to cry.

"I'll heat a bottle." Bea said and left me alone in the living room.

I lowered myself on the flowered couch with lace doilies protecting the arms and back. Loosening Noel's snowsuit, I pulled her close while pushing the discarded clothing to the floor. I kissed her forehead and rocked her rhythmically to stop her crying. Bea quietly entered the room and handed me the warm

bottle. With her finger to her lips, she stood for a moment then left. Noel sucked greedily on the bottle. Gradually, Noel drifted off to sleep, jerking occasionally and waving her tiny fingers. Then she renewed her sucking until I eventually pulled the bottle gently from her and set it on the side table beside a stack of books. They were mostly Harlequin novels, but one I noticed was called, 'How To Stay Young All Your Life' by Clement G. Martin, MD. I carefully pulled it closer and read all of the claims it made to change your life. Bea, it seemed, was interested in 'How to make your sex life more meaningful.'

I laughed. This didn't fit the image I'd developed of her. Remembering her words on the front porch moments ago, I tried to imagine the people waiting anxiously to receive my daughter but it hurt too much. So instead I stared at my baby and tried to memorize her face for all time.

I wondered, *Do you understand what's going on? Will you notice when I stop coming*? The next day I would sign the adoption papers, which would turn my angel over to a life with strangers. *Will you think of me when you're growing up*? I touched her little cheek.

"You have my eyes. I wonder if you will look like me? Or think of me and wonder, or will they never tell you that you were adopted?" I whispered. "I wish I could keep you. Run away, just the two of us, but I have nothing to offer you."

My tears hit her cheek and she started to whimper. "Shoo, shoo, little baby, don't you cry."

I sat for hours that last afternoon, holding Noel saying good-bye, rocking, swaying, singing ever so quietly. I didn't want Bea to hear me. It was too personal, too private and too stupid. I sang these words to my Noel, even though in my heart I knew I would never see her again once I signed the papers.

"There's a place for us, a time and place for us". The words from West Side Story generated a significance that would stay with me forever, "we'll find a new way of living, we'll find a way of forgiving". Singing and dreaming, during that last private moment, "there's a place for us, a time and place for us, sometime, somehow."

I KEPT THOSE photos the foster mother took for years, taking them out when I was alone and allowing myself to think of her. How was she? Was she happy? Were her adoptive parents good to her? Did she live in a nice home amongst a happy family? I would stare at her image and wonder. *Is she pretty? Does she look like me? Or her father? Did she go to university?*

I kept track of each birthday. I imagined her celebrating her sweet sixteenth. Was it good or was she confused and mixed up like me at that age? *Is she in love? And if so, what is he like, this boy whom my baby loves? Does he know how lucky he is? Do her parents know? Do they understand the magnitude of the gift of my baby?*

Christmases came and went. The yearning started each December with the carol, The First Noel. My emotions

mushroomed until her birthday in February so that by the time the day arrived, there were no tears left.

I would hold her photo and wish things had been different. I put the photographs away, well hidden in a bottom drawer, knowing they were there each time I passed. One letter to tell me she was okay, alive and well, healthy and happy was all I needed.

CHAPTER 11

WE PULLED UP to the drab, post-war municipal building that held the Juvenile Courthouse and parked. Mom got out of the car. I lingered, not wanting to go. If I just sat there, maybe it wouldn't happen.

"Come," was all she said. Feeling powerless, I followed her inside.

The halls were bleak, their walls dulled with age. Water marks stained parts of the ceiling and there was a slight musty odor. Grey and white squares of linoleum lay chipped and worn at our feet. We sat on a hard wooden bench outside Courtroom number 3.

My thoughts drifted back to the day my mother and aunts took me to the main courthouse in downtown Toronto to see where my grandfather had presided as a magistrate.

WE HAD SEARCHED for my grandfather's portrait among the paintings of past judges and Mom bragged how respected he had been. We were all so proud when we looked up at his majestic face. My mother told me how he sometimes helped the people he convicted, bringing them home to work odd jobs after they had been released because no one else would employ an ex-convict.

The courthouse had a grand entryway, arched ceilings and marble pillars. There was none of that grandeur here.

As I recalled the visit and my grandfather's legacy, I felt so ashamed. Was he looking down at us from heaven? Did he know the shame I had brought to the family? Surely, it was my father's blood, raging through my veins, that had brought me to this. Clenching my teeth, I pushed my body hard against the bench in an effort to disappear. It was here that I would give my baby away and, with her, an essential part of myself.

I thought of holding my Noel yesterday, saying good-bye with her wide eyes looking up at me so innocently. I had given the social worker a poem to send to her new parents.

MONDAYS' CHILD IS FAIR OF FACE
TUESDAY'S CHILD IS FULL OF GRACE

WEDNESDAY'S CHILD IS LOVING AND GIVING

THURSDAY'S CHILD WORKS HARD FOR A LIVING

FRIDAY'S CHILD IS FULL OF WOE
SATURDAYS CHILD HAS FAR TO GO

BUT THE CHILD THAT IS BORN ON THE SABBATH DAY

IS BRAVE AND BONNY GOOD AND GAY

Noel was born on a Sunday.

I TOUCHED MY mother's arm and pleaded in one last desperate attempt to stop the events from unfolding. "Please don't make me do this."

"Don't start." She sat stiffly in her black dress, her court attire, as though she was at a funeral. She was - mine.

Mom insisted that I wear the new white dress she had bought me as though by wearing it I would become a virgin again, that by signing my baby away, to strangers, my life could return to the way it had been. Of course, I knew it would never be the same.

I was too young to be an adult but too full of life's experiences to be a child, a woman/child trapped outside the boundaries of both. An outcast robbed of childhood laughter, yet too young to enjoy the control of adulthood. I longed to be held, cared for and told everything would be all right.

"I'll get a job. I'll take care of her." Mom and I never used Noel's name openly. It was always 'her' to Mom so as not to get too personal. Not to imagine her as my daughter or my mother's granddaughter.

"You have to go back to school."

"I'll go to school at night and work during the day."

"What kind of a job could you get? No dear, this is best for you and the baby."

Before I could argue my case any further, the courtroom doors opened and the bailiff called my name. His voice echoed through the empty hallway. I sat frozen. Mother stood and walked toward the doors yanking on my arm, forcing me to follow.

I knew nothing of duress at that age or that I wasn't old enough to sign a legal contract, so when the judge asked me if I

understood what I was doing, I could only nod and mumble a leaden yes.

THERE ARE MOMENTS in time, frozen, but never forgotten. This was the day my heart froze. It was the only way I could survive. Un-empowered, intimidated, I let them take my Noel.

I left the courthouse with a soul as deadened as any of those women in the doll's eyeball factory. My tears dried. I put my girlish dreams away. No more fairy tales of pumpkins turned into carriages and white knights to carry me off. Life had dished me a healthy dose of reality so I pushed my dream of Noel where no one would see, only allowing myself to think about her occasionally, like a precious jewel removed from the vault where I could view the purity and the beauty, but only for a moment.

CHAPTER 12

GOING BACK TO school terrified me.

My brother, Doug helped me confront my fear. I was still working at the doll factory when he came home from university for the summer, four months after Noel's birth.

There are determining moments in everyone's life. A conversation we had was one of those moments. Without that talk, I might have stayed at the factory but Doug gave me back a feeling of self-worth.

He never openly approached the topic of my pregnancy. The family pretended he didn't know. Instead, he talked about a girl he had gone to high school with and how she went back to school after she had given a baby up for adoption. "She held her head up high and walked into school the following September."

How stupid the whole thing was - a conversation about me, but not about me.

"Sure, somebody might have talked behind her back, but most of the people I know respected her for it." Doug continued.

There was no way we could communicate openly back then, yet his story gave me the courage I needed and sustained me when I felt like quitting. It took every bit of nerve I possessed to walk into school that fall. I probably did it more for Doug than for myself.

I knew my situation was a major source of gossip. Walking through the school corridors, I could hear whispers and observe the judgment on the faces of many of the students, but remembering Doug's words, I held my head high no matter how frightened or alone I felt. By rising to his challenge, I hoped to gain his respect but more importantly, I came to respect myself. Proud of the adversity I had overcome.

Looking back, I wonder how my life would have turned out had I never gotten pregnant. Lots of girls had sex back then but I was the one who got 'caught'. If I didn't, would I have remained the party girl I was as a teenager? Or would I have made something of my life anyways? After all, I was a strong, determined girl long before I had Noel. The guidance counsellor in grade school told my parents I should only take secretarial courses in high school and Mom and Dad tried to convince me to oblige. I fought them, even at the young age of twelve, determined to stick to academic studies so I could go to university. I believe schools had a quota in the Sixties, allocating percentages to secretarial, shop and academic.. No way I'd let them choose for me even back then. As well, I lied about my age to get a job at thirteen, before the legal working age, so I could buy the beautiful clothes I wanted instead of wearing hand-me-downs from my cousins. I did have a strong will so perhaps I would have been just as successful without this determining crossroad. I'll never know.

MY PREVIOUS SCHOOLMATES had moved up a grade. So as an older, scandalous student, I didn't have much in common with the kids in my class. I became a loner determined to get an education. *Screw them all.* I threw myself into studying.

My grades were good but in the end, not good enough. After graduating, I received this letter from Ryerson, the post secondary institution I'd applied for:

'Although you have the grades, due to the popularity of Early Childhood Education, we must turn down your application at this time. Please reapply next year.'

It was the only post secondary school I had applied to. There was nothing else I wanted to study and it was too late to apply elsewhere anyway, so I quit school and started an array of jobs, promoting tourism in Florida, various sales positions, an assistant occupational therapist. I even drove a truck delivering lobster tanks. I never stayed at one position for long. Work was only a means to save money to travel.

At nineteen, I left home abruptly when a girl asked me to share her apartment. Mom cried a lot and brought me cooked chicken and vitamins. By then, our relationship had changed dramatically. In fact, I reversed our relationship by appointing myself my mother's keeper, focusing on my feelings of superiority. In my eyes, she was a victim of her marriage

and my father played the role of villain, an image my mother worked hard at instilling. I vowed I would never allow a man to treat me like he did her. I argued with my father on her behalf although she never asked me to. I did things she never dreamed of doing then relished relaying my experiences to brighten her boring life.

For the rest of her life, she continually told me, "You are so brave. I could never do that," referring to my jobs or my travels. Perhaps Mom viewed the new life I established for myself as a strength she lacked, as though I had escaped and she hadn't. Now, instead of hating her, I felt sorry for her and wanted to protect her. The overbearing role I took on, must have been painful for her at times but I was too self-absorbed with my own emotional survival to consider hers.

Until she died, my mother and I never discussed the winter of 1965 to 1966. I suppressed my anger to a place deep inside me, determined to take back control of my own destiny.

There are so many questions, now years after her death that I wish I could ask about those days I hid in the basement. Were you protecting me from a cruel world? Or yourself? What did you really feel? Did you think about your lost granddaughter? How I would love to have a long chat over tea.

As for me, I became the invincible super woman. I thought I would die when I lost my daughter but I didn't, so I decided I could survive anything. Nothing or no one would ever hurt me again. Not money, work, my parents, a man, nothing. I needed no one. This tough shell protected me well over the years.

CHAPTER 13

DOUG DIED. IT was 1972, one month before my twenty-second birthday.

He was completing his P.H.D. while working at the head office of the Bank of Montreal managing the bank's investments. At the time of his death, he was married and had James, his one- year-old son. For months prior to his death, his doctors could not diagnose what was making him ill. A simple ear infection wouldn't heal and destroyed all but 10% of his hearing in one ear.

"It's better than going blind," he joked, laughing as he switched off his hearing aids, teasing his wife that she talked too much. After several months of treatment, the drugs failed to arrest the symptoms. His legs swelled and he had trouble walking, so his puzzled doctors hospitalized him for observation.

He asked me to move to Montreal and help his wife, Claudia, with the baby after he was admitted to hospital. We kept his illness a secret from my parents. The doctor assured us he would be hale and hearty in no time, yet still couldn't diagnose his mysterious illness.

Anytime Mom and Dad called, his wife or I would tell them Doug was working late or out or asleep. Then we would call Doug at the hospital and he would phone them back. It felt horrible, so I asked him why he insisted on the secrecy.

"I don't want to upset them." Doug said. "And they would want to visit. They can't afford the trip." He also confessed that it would be too much for his wife to have them staying at their house while she was trying to cope with a one year old and visiting the hospital twice a day.

My parent's thirtieth wedding anniversary passed, with neither, Doug or I travelling to Toronto to attend the celebration. I can't remember what excuse we used. I can imagine how our absence must have hurt them, but I honored my brother's request. Wish I hadn't. My parents never saw their son again.

My handsome brother's moon face started to bloat and became puffy and pale. His alert blue eyes were dull and droopy. His blonde hair thinned dramatically. The staff was too busy to help him shower as often as he liked and he refused to let me assist him. Doug had always taken good care of his body, continuing a rigid air force exercise regime since his time in the armed forces. He was extremely concerned about gangrene setting in. His legs discolored since he became bed ridden. Still he tried not to worry me and continually thanked me for coming to Montreal to help out.

Three other patients shared Doug's hospital ward. One bed was occupied by a man withdrawing from heroin. His arms and legs were secured to the guardrails of his bed. He was drenched in sweat and howled in constant pain. It was an intolerable environment for my brother. It took a few days of persistent trips to the nurse's station to have the man removed to a private room. The other patient's moaning seemed inconsequential once the drug addict was removed. I sat for hours by my brother's bedside. One day we opened up to each other.

No one ever talked in my family, but finally Doug and I did. He would never approach the subject of Noel himself but he appeared relieved when I did.

"You gave me the strength to carry on."

"I did?" Doug responded.

"Remember the story you told me when you came home from university the summer after I gave birth? About the girl who returned to school after a teen pregnancy?"

"Of course." He answered. "Mom made me swear I would never embarrass you, but I couldn't allow you to continue to work in that horrible factory."

"Yeah." I frowned remembering the poor women who worked there. "Your story gave me my life back." His face lit up.

He leaned forward to place his arms on my shoulders. "It makes me happy that my story helped but I'm positive you

wouldn't have settled for a life in that factory. You would have done it on your own eventually." Doug squeezed my hand and continued, "You did the right thing you know. You say I gave you your life but you gave your baby a life. You couldn't raise her on your own. You gave her the greatest gift you could, a father and a mother."

"She has a name. Noel." It felt good to say her name out loud.

"Noel," Doug repeated her name thoughtfully. "Noel, beautiful. I'm very proud of you and have always wanted to tell you so." He punched my arm, "You're tough."

"I am now." I answered leaning into his embrace. "Don't have clue where I'm going though." Sighing I confessed to my brother, "My last relationship was a disaster."

"Oh," Doug leaned forward, "tell me."

"His name was Wally. We were living together in Edmonton."

"Ah ha." Doug laughed. "Claudia and I suspected as much when you said you didn't have a phone. Yeah, right, your age and no phone. Not likely."

"Dad would have had a fit if he knew. Anyway, I moved to Edmonton because of Wally and if he had asked me to marry him, I would have in a minute but he didn't. Thank God. We moved in together and I got to see that marriage was a whole lot different from the movies. He was handsome and successful. You would have liked him. He was a man's man –

athletic, intelligent but, was he anal. Everything in his apartment was placed precisely and not to be moved. Everything was black and white except his green shag wall-to-wall carpet. I raked that carpet every day, backing myself into the kitchen where I'd experiment with gourmet cooking. But no matter how clean I kept the place, Wally found fault. He'd come in and run his finger on the top of paintings to ensure I'd dusted the frame."

"Really?"

"Yes really. I even cleaned the toilet bowl every day and did laundry every other day cos he wouldn't use a towel twice. I told him I was going to Toronto to visit Mom and Dad, but I never intended to return. I don't believe in a prince in shining armor any more. Gave up that fantasy years ago."

Doug hugged me. "One day, someone will be very lucky to marry you."

"Yeah, well I'm not counting on it. So if I never get married, I'm going to have to take care of myself, I need some sort of a career."

"I'm sure you'll figure it out."

When I stood to leave, not knowing I would never see him conscious again, he touched my face lovingly and told me, "I finally feel as though we are family." I threw my arms around his neck and we hugged quietly for a long time before I pulled myself away so I could relieve my sister-in-law with the

baby. When I turned to wave from the door, he dabbed his eyes and reached for the Kleenex beside his bed.

The following day, he slipped into a coma.

One of the most difficult things I've ever had to do was to phone my parents and tell them Doug was in hospital in a coma. How we must have hurt them. They cried but didn't blame me.

The call came from the hospital at 3a.m.. Doug had died and we were needed to come immediately to sign autopsy papers. It was only then, that the doctors determined he had a rare disease of the arteries called periarteritis nodosa. The actual cause of death was from the heavy dosages of Prednisone, a steroid that damaged his stomach and caused the walls to burst.

In the morning I phoned my parents.

Not once did I imagine his death as a possible outcome. In the five years since I gave Noel up for adoption, I hadn't thought I could harden further but I was wrong. Throughout his memorial service on that sunny June day, standing beside my grieving parents, I could not cry.

He had been such a high achiever with so many dreams. We were robbed of his vibrancy. He was only twenty-eight.

I remained in Montreal for six months to help Claudia with my nephew. During the months before Doug died, I experienced his son's first step and coherent words. Now I watched him grow more each day. I would sit on the bathroom

floor and sing words of encouragement during potty training, walk him if he cried, wipe mushy baby goo off his face and out of his hair when he played with his food.

Claudia and I took him to the Hotel Bonaventure for their Mother's Day buffet. The hostess gave me the Mother's Day rose, which upset both Claudia and I for different reasons. I privately longed to be the mother and my heart ached as it often did during my times caring for my nephew. The newborn baby scent was gone, replaced sometimes by smelly diapers or the remnants of his last meal but I loved it all and yearned for Noel. I wondered how she was. She would be six now and starting a full day of school. Had she been frightened? Did her new mother walk her to school? Were her parents still together or divorced? It tormented me to think my daughter might be raised by a single mother, after all.

When James took his afternoon naps and Claudia was busy clearing up Doug's estate, I would sit quietly for hours flipping through dusty photo albums, pondering the meaning of life. I studied photos of Doug standing proudly beside the cockpit of the small bomber plane he captained for the Air Force or the expression of pure joy as he held his son. I would stare at his intelligent smiling face in photos of him posing regally in his red uniform when he graduated from military college.

People really died. I would die. The stark realization, generated questions. How did I want my life to look? Given

that I may never marry, what work would I do to support myself? I needed something more than the transient life I was leading. I needed purpose. Doug's death inspired the determination I needed. I registered for university.

CHAPTER 14

IN 1973 THE University of Toronto required all returning 'mature' students to complete a summer long, pre-university course, in either, English, Math or Science and attain a 80% grade. I chose English. At the end of the grueling term, the professor only gave me 79% and told me I should start off with part-time courses. I brought him a rosy apple and argued my case. He wouldn't budge so I went to the school counselor's office who backed the prof's decision. Undeterred, I approached the Dean. I knew my level of commitment was strong enough to succeed. I insisted on full-time registration and reluctantly, he agreed.

Being older than the other undergraduate students, I kept to myself and concentrated on achieving decent marks. I completed the four-year program in three, graduating with a B+ average in commerce and communications. Proudly, I proved them all wrong.

As well as my normal studies, I also worked full time in the evenings. Still obsessed with travelling, I took advantage of the long summer breaks to travel. The first summer, after touring Cambridge and Ely, in the English countryside, I arrived in London without a job. I intended to hit all the major hotels.

The Hilton was my first stop. I told the woman in the Personal Department that I would make beds, scrub floors, whatever they wanted. I was delighted when she offered me the prestigious position of hostess in their main dining room.

My first day on the job, the manager drilled me as to who were regular, important guests. A certain Lord ate lunch there every Tuesday. "Make sure you seat him at table 8 by the window," he said. "A group of socialite wives come in for cocktails and appetizers after their weekly bridge game. They get be a little rowdy so I always place them in the far corner."

"Also Enrique Martell from The Philippines comes to the hotel several times a year. He is staying with us now and likes to be seated here." He pointed to the table near the entry where I stood.

So when a tall, obviously Filipino man, walked in and went straight to that particular table, it didn't take a genius to figure out who he was.

"Hello Mr. Martell. My name is Margaret and I just started working with the Hilton today. Pleased to meet you." I held out my hand.

He looked up from his newspaper, stood and bowed slightly while smoothing his perfectly pressed blue suit. Then he took my hand and held it in a firm grip. His hands were large and slightly callused but his nails were perfectly manicured. He was tall for a Filipino, 6'2". I soon learned he was half Spanish. He was dark skinned. His ebony hair was slicked back and he had a

moustache. Soft slate eyes sparkled, revealing how much he enjoyed being recognized.

Enrique Martell generally took all three meals at the hotel which was when I worked. The room I shared with three strangers at the Earl's Court Home for Young Women, turned off the phones and the hot water from ten in the evening until seven in the morning. I began my workday with the breakfast shift so I needed to arrive early in order to shower at the hotel before starting. My hours formally ended after lunch at two thirty each afternoon but I jumped at the chance to work the dinner shift as well. London was expensive and I needed to work as much as possible to cover the rent, the cost of my tube pass and leave some money to subsidize my university expenses that exceeded the student loans I was accumulating.

As I stood beside Mr. Martell several times each day, we started the first of many easy conversations. After several weeks, he announced, "I need a secretary to travel with me. Are you interested?"

It wasn't the first proposition I'd received from the Hilton's male clientele.

"Thank you very much, Mr. Martell, but I'm happy with my employment here."

"If you change your mind, let me know."

EACH AFTERTOON, BETWEEN the lunch and dinner crowds, I would sit with several of the staff and enjoy anything I wanted

on the menu. I mostly chose a fine port and stilton cheese. That afternoon, I told the manager about Martell's job offer.

"It is true he's looking for a secretary. The head concierge told me he has been interviewing girls from a placement agency all week."

"Sure, but,"

My face must have indicated my cynicism, because he cut me off saying, "Mr. Martell has been coming to this hotel for several years and I have never seen him with a woman. If he offered you a job, he meant just that, a job."

I phoned his room that evening and asked if we could discuss the job further. We met the next day, for afternoon tea, at the Four Seasons Hotel.

"I NEED SOMEONE to arrange my airline tickets. I travel all over the world, often changing destinations, which requires someone to spend hours at airline offices. It's a waste of my time when I'm doing business. Also I require some typing. You do type don't you?"

"Of course." I answered, relieved that I had taken a secretarial course after high school even though I hated the one office job I tried. Hopefully, I could still type.

"I will pay you $500 US a month and all of your expenses."

Being paid to travel! I almost choked on my scone and clotted cream. For a student, in 1974, that was a dream job, but I needed to be honest, "I'm going back to university in the fall."

"Oh."

"Yes, I go home to Toronto in three months."

"Well, let's give it a try and see how you feel in September. If you want to go home, I'll find someone else."

"Perfect."

"It's settled then. And please from now on call me Henry." He extended his hand which I shook. "We're leaving for Germany on Friday."

"Oh no, I can't. I have to give notice to the hotel."

"Don't worry, I'll take care of that."

"It's only fair to give them at least one week."

"Okay, if that's what you want. I'll be back from Germany on Wednesday. We'll leave for New York the following weekend." He pulled out his wallet. "Here's five hundred dollars to pay any rent or other expenses you may have in order to leave so quickly." As though the rat hole I was living in required any notice.

He then pulled out two, hundred-pound notes, "And buy yourself a new outfit. You've worn that same dress every day."

I waved the money away, laughing, "It's my uniform."

"Oh, that explains it." Enrique laughed. "Still," he pushed the money towards me, "you'll need some new items I'm sure. I'll make arrangements at the hotel for you."

That's how I went from living in a seedy boarding house and working at the hotel to being checked into a suite next door to Mr. Martell.

Yes, the staff did talk.

I TELEPHONED MY mother to tell her about my new job and that I would be flying to New York City the next week.

"How exciting. You're so brave to travel like that and make new friends."

She didn't express any concern about me going off with a stranger.

"I'll try to come home for the weekend if I can," I promised. But, in the morning Enrique and I rode down in the elevator together. When we got on, we were travelling to New York, but by the time we reached the lobby, he had changed our itinerary to Tokyo. "I'm needed there more."

That was life with Enrique Martell. He owned a steel conglomerate in Manila, busy with government contracts, a Sheraton hotel and paper manufacturing. Mostly, he followed his freighters around the world organizing cargo.

Our first stop was to his Tokyo office. We checked into adjoining suites at the Imperial Palace Hotel. It was situated across from the Emperor's palace and gardens and had been designed by Frank Lloyd Wright. It reflected the architect's fascination with Asian design. The stark concrete walls of the entryway were softened by meditation gardens of raked gravel and a solitary rock representing the moon. Business men congregated for drinks in the huge lobby where I imagined multinational deals were being negotiated. The manager rushed over to greet us personally and delivered fruit, cheese and flowers

to our rooms, both gorgeous suites with separate living and sleeping rooms.

The furnishings were magnificent in their simplicity. A tall hand painted vase was highlighted in a small alcove. Enrique told me that the vase was probably valued around $30,000. The Japanese admired artisans who spent a lifetime perfecting their craft of pottery, sword making, watercolors and such. I fell in love with their woodblock prints and bought several because they were inexpensive. The Japanese didn't value the prints as an art form and even used them to wrap and ship pottery until the giijin (foreigners) discovered them.

My suite was a corner room with one window overlooking an ancient Kabuki theatre where Enrique explained that only men were allowed to perform the various roles. During our stay in Tokyo, I often went to see the performances there. The other window was covered in a window box filled with beautiful foliage. The Japanese called these artificial views, 'Borrowed scenery'.

The lower level of the hotel was an underground mall filled with expensive boutiques and Japanese restaurants serving sushi, teriyaki or delicacies such as Shabu Shabu or Sukiyaki cooked right at the table by beautiful women dressed in colorful kimonos.

My job was pretty basic. I typed a few letters, arranged luncheons with clients and delivered letters and gifts. In the evening, we dined together at the best restaurants where the entire staff would stop whatever they were doing and bow to us

while calling out welcome in Japanese when we entered. Enrique introduced me to ancient Geisha houses and private key clubs where six foot bouquets of flowers often adorned the rooms. He told me that the Japanese Mafia forced the owners to buy flowers each week as a way to pay them for protection. The smell of fresh flowers filled the dim lit rooms while the large bouquets also hid comfortable couches to enhance privacy. Women in kimonos danced to entertain us and were trained in the ancient art of making their guests feel magnificent. Several beautiful women would gush over me and Enrique then the geishas would quietly rotate one by one so as not to be noticeable when they moved on to a new table. They would touch my blonde hair with fascination and ask endless questions, disappointed when I told them I loved the Japanese Shiseido make-up line and not some American brand, which to them was exotic. Several geishas would flirt with Enrique whose six-foot-two frame towered over them. He actually looked a little embarrassed if I momentarily ignored my own pampering and glanced over. A geisha would kneel at our feet and ensure our sake or Santory whiskey never emptied.

Enrique told me there were bars in Tokyo, which specialized in young boys who were available for sex if the female clientele wanted to hire them for the night. I wondered if he was letting me know where to get sex if I needed it. Once he took me to a transvestite bar where men dressed as beautiful women. One asked me to dance then touched my breasts and said, 'Lucky' in English before signaling to several other transvestites to come and

feel me up. Enrique held his sides in laughter when I rushed back to the table beet red and said it was time to leave.

I giggled constantly and was generally a little tipsy, but Enrique, always the perfect gentleman, never tried to take advantage of my inebriation. I became quite addicted to hot sake, and also loved the strong flavor of Santory whiskey and the delightful sensation as it warmed my insides going down, until the hotel doctor advised me sake was too strong for Western metabolisms, when I complained about a continued upset stomach.

Enrique confessed that he had traveled alone for so many years that he was no longer interested in sightseeing, but he delighted in my enthusiastic discovery of Japan. He would insist that I take time to explore Tokyo or take day excursions to Kamakura or Nikko. Then he would smile as I recounted every detail over dinner.

He arranged a trip for me to Kyoto, the ancient capital of Japan while he flew to Manila for a few days. I stayed in a traditional Japanese inn on the river and walked for miles exploring the historic shrines and temples. When I returned to Tokyo the following rainy Sunday, I ordered room service and invited Enrique to join me for a picnic which I had set out on the bedspread I had laid out on the floor. There was a Japanese attempt at French bread, Brie, Kobe beef prized by the Japanese because the cows were massaged regularly and fed beer or sake to tenderize the meat. The crème de la crème was a specialty melon where only two melons were allowed to grow on each plant so that

the fruit was especially sweet. One melon cost $10US in 1973 and had risen to $50 by 1979. To accompany the fruit and satisfy Henry's sweet tooth, I also ordered an array of petit fours which like the baguette, would not impress any French chef.

We watched Japanese television while we ate and Enrique laughed as I made up my own story to go with the movie we were watching. I had to change the plot constantly when it didn't follow the story line I had invented. Enrique eventually joined in the fun and added his own twist to the stories.

After our meal, I set up my new cassette player with music I had bought in Kyoto. He clapped with delight while I danced a traditional geisha dance. To complete the performance, I wore the used kimono I had purchased in Tokyo. It was hand painted with gold stitching. The previous owner's name was embroidered in Japanese symbols at the back of the neck. Enrique clapped for a full five minutes while I continued to bow proudly. I gushed with details about Kyoto and Nara, explaining how while standing outside an ancient temple, I'd watched several women practice the dance. They caught me peeking and, giggling, pulled me inside, insisting I sit on a cushion and watch them perform. When I stood to mimic their movements, they placed their hands delicately over their mouths and laughed wholeheartedly. Then without speaking the language, they patiently taught me the steps until I managed to perform it in its entirety. I communicated that I needed the name of the music, which I immediately went out and bought.

Despite his business acumen and wealth, Enrique was a shy man and would likely have maintained a strictly professional relationship, but I had become enraptured by his sincere manner. So when I finished my dance, I handed him a thank you card, then leaned over and kissed him. I felt his surprise as I pressed my lips to his. I didn't let go of my hold around his neck. He soon responded with all the pent up passion of someone who had been alone too long. When I pulled away, he gave me a questioning look and smiled shyly. How could I resist this sweet man who had swept me from my suburban life and given me the world? I seduced him right there on the hotel carpet amid the remnants of our picnic.

"You didn't have to have sex with me, you know." He told me after. "I was happy with just your company."

"I know Henry. If I thought I had to have sex with you, I wouldn't be here. I wanted to. You've been so nice, I couldn't resist you."

Henry, as I was now comfortable calling him, held me close as he told me about his first and only love. As a young man, he had left Manila to study at MIT in Boston. He planned to return and marry his childhood sweetheart but while he was away, she married someone else. He never got over her and threw himself into building his empire.

"I don't have a lot of experience with women."

As far as I was concerned, he had no need to worry.

I moved into his suite and Henry blossomed like a young teenager in love. He would burst into song, singing romantic Spanish songs to me in taxis or restaurants.

"Years ago, I hired an entire orchestra to accompany me singing outside my girlfriend's window," he told me. His favourite song which he dedicated to me was 'Quizas, quizas, quizas' which he translated as 'you think, you think, you think....too much".

Henry started to join me on my excursions into the Japanese countryside and when I told him my twenty-fourth birthday was the following weekend, he became very excited.

"I will think up something very special."

We were staying in Sasebo on the southern island of Kushu while one of his freighters was being dry docked. He woke me early Saturday morning and told me to pack an overnight case. A taxi was waiting which drove us south into Unzen National Park. At a small turn in the road, Enrique told the driver to turn left and the car climbed high into the mountains where we stopped at a creek side restaurant for a picnic Japanese style. Cokes signs strung together by wire swung in the breeze between pine trees whose fresh scent was like a spray of room freshener.

"You told me you liked soba." Henry beamed.

"Love it." I would often buy a dish of the noodles at the small Ma and Pop wagons which were rolled out on to the sidewalks of the Ginza each evening.

"This is a very famous place for soba." He led me amongst the trees where several round metal vats were set up as tables and surrounded by chairs. "The Japanese are ingenious at inventing

new ways for everything," he pointed to the hoses leading from the stream to the vats. "They direct the fresh mountain water into these vats." He held his hand up to the waiter who came over and placed cooked soba noodles in the water.

"You grab the noodles then dip them in several different sauces. They're delicious." Henry insisted our taxi driver join us for lunch and they laughed together watching me try to catch hold of the noodles with my chop sticks as they swirled by in the cold mountain water. Birds chirped loudly as the stream gurgled past us, both providing the perfect musical accompaniment.

That night we stopped in an ancient Ryokan style inn where the Japanese Prime Minister had stayed the month before. Our driver slept in a small room at the back of the hotel while Henry reserved the suite for us. In the morning, we went for breakfast in a restaurant overlooking magnificent Japanese gardens, as beautiful Japanese women dressed in magnificent kimonos waited on us.

"Oh," I pointed disappointed, "there should be tables in the garden. It's so beautiful.

Henry immediately held up his hand and waved to one of the waitresses standing close. He explained what he wanted and within minutes our table was placed in the middle of the garden while the female staff giggled endlessly behind their raised hands and the men winked. This was my romantic Henry. I fell in love with the excitement, the glamour and something I had only observed but never experienced firsthand, the power of money.

This was global wealth which no one in my family had ever had. I loved every minute of it.

We spent summers together over the next several years. Travel changes who you are. I realized I could now travel anywhere, live anywhere, meet strangers and adjust to any city in the world. I felt free and laughed outright when one of my aunts wrote to me in Japan and demanded that I come home from that awful country. She was still living with memories of World War Two. Now, I felt as worldly as any of my cousins. There was nothing I couldn't do or have if I wanted it.

"I'M SORRY, I can't." I told Henry as we sat in the parking lot of the new cultural centre built on reclaimed land in Manila. It was a strange place to propose marriage but we had been in The Philippines for a few days and I must have passed some test when his family appeared to accept me. Being staunch Catholics, I stayed with his brother and sister-in-law. Olga laughed when I made my own bed but I quickly adapted to having one servant polish my nails while another brought me freshly squeezed juice or brushed my hair. The family of four, had nine live-in servants, one who was trained to give massages every day. I thought a live-in masseur was the peak of decadence although I admit that Henry and I often had two masseurs come to our hotel room in Tokyo for a massage before sleeping.

He lived with his mother in the house they shared in Makarti.

"I bet you don't even type." His frail eighty year old mother exclaimed. Her dark, sun drenched skin wrinkled in laughter as she tapped my hand with her fan. Each sister-in-law admitted Henry would be angry with them but they took turns drilling me anyway at the Polo Park Country Club.

Henry had three brothers. One was married to the sister of Imelda Marcos, wife of the President of The Philippines who sent his regrets that he was too busy with the Miss Universe contest to meet with me on this trip. Another brother was married to Etelka, a Dutch woman who warned me that mothers in The Philippines were not allowed to raise their own children. She had a nanny for each child. Her role was to kiss them good morning and good night and had little to do with their upbringing.

So when we sat in the car the night he proposed, I knew I couldn't marry him. I loved Henry but knew I couldn't adapt to his lifestyle.

"Don't go back to the University of Toronto. Study at the University of the Philippines. It's a great facility."

"What good is an education if I can't use my degree?"

"Martell women don't work."

"Teach me the shipping business."

He just patted my head and laughed.

"The captain of the Maru asked me to go to Madagascar in the state cabin." I told him. "I'd like to go."

"Are you crazy? Let you go on a ship with a bunch of horny sailors? No way." Henry shook his head adamantly. "You wouldn't be safe."

"They wouldn't dare be inappropriate with the boss's girlfriend."

"No, you'll join the country club. Take up mahjong or tennis like the other wives. Tear down my house and the one next door. Build what you want."

"And what about your mother? She lives there too."

"She will live with us, of course."

"I don't think I can adapt to your lifestyle in Manila."

"Then travel with me."

"For months on end? What would I do all day if you won't let me learn the shipping business?"

"Then, I'll buy you a house in Tokyo and London. Fix them up."

He looked so sincere and willing to do anything to make me stay. Anything except allow me my own career. I loved this man. Who couldn't? He was kind and generous.

"As much as I love travelling, I can't be a gypsy twelve months a year. I need to work." I touched his sad face, "I would only divorce you in five years and take half your money. I care for you too much to do that."

I CONTINUED TO meet up with Henry somewhere in the world over the next several years. On one trip, he told me he was in a camera shop in Manila when he saw a young Filipino ogling an expensive camera. He asked the fellow if he was going to buy it? The young man said he couldn't afford to buy the camera because

he was moving to Toronto with his family. His face dropped when he watched Henry call the clerk over and pay the $1000 for the camera of his dreams. Henry then turned to the young Filipino, a perfect stranger, and handed him the camera. The man was flabbergasted and tried to push it back saying he could never pay him back. Henry said, “I don’t want you to. All I ask is that when you are in Toronto and you see a Filipino in trouble, you help him.” Then Henry turned and walked out of the store.

I LOOK BACK on Henry as my fairy tale. He gave me the world. I could have had everything my aunts had and more but his gift to me was understanding that money was not what I needed. I wanted to share a life, do something useful and most of all I wanted to raise a child with the man I loved. I lost my Noel, so how could I agree to let nannies raise my children? I cared deeply for this man but I didn’t love him enough.

IT WAS THE Seventies – an era of free love and I did enjoy other men over the years but nothing like some of the female friends I knew, who insisted they were liberated and could have as many lovers as men did. I was not such a free spirit and toyed with the men I dated. Always in control, I picked men who adored me while knowing I could walk away any time.

Before Henry, at university, there had been Alexis, who claimed to be a descendant of Russian aristocracy. Dark, good looking, bright, well-educated but incapable of living in the

present world. He should have been a gentleman farmer or a gigolo. Women loved him instantly, attracted to his Bohemian spirit. All too quickly, they, myself included, would learn that he was too idealistic. The myth of his ancestry held him back. He completed his architectural degree but seldom worked. He had no bank account nor any credit card. Of course, he also had no money. He considered himself an anarchist and made sure the government could never trace his whereabouts, not that he ever did anything which needed hiding. Opposed to divorce, he never married, preferring to live with a series of women. An ideal which somehow complied to his idealism and justified his lack of commitment.

But what a lover! He specialized in sex in a way that only the truly unemployed have time to do. He played at love making, setting the scene with food, wine and music, cooking extravagant meals while donning only an apron. Or he would wear a raincoat and chase me flashing until I let him catch me. He helped me to laugh again and explore my sexuality. A romantic who could delight my body but not be taken seriously. He needed a playmate, not a life partner. The woman who settled for Alexis would have to forfeit security for great sex. I needed someone with more ambition.

Then there was Jerry. Stable boring Jerry. I called him my in-between boyfriend. Jerry reappeared conveniently when one man left and before I opened the door to another. He was a little overweight with a constant sheen of sweat on his upper lip. I couldn't bear to kiss him. He had a warm, pleasant look, dark

curly hair, sparkling brown eyes and a friendly smile. He would do anything to please me, dinners in the finest restaurants, driving to Niagara-on-the-Lake at midnight for liqueurs.

God, how I wished I could love him. My parents did. My friends loved him. Who wouldn't? He was successful, kind, funny. In his eyes, I was a princess. No, a queen! But I was too strong for Jerry. I wanted to love him but could not imagine waking up to him every morning. No, I couldn't settle for marrying Jerry.

I enjoyed my freedom and prided myself on not needing a man to feel fulfilled. Had I become so self absorbed and independent that I was incapable of loving anyone? I wasn't unhappy. I loved my life, playing at various jobs as a means to tour the world. There was no time for seriousness. That was until Christmas 1978.

CHAPTER 15

SHE DIED, IN my arms, on Christmas Day.

I believed my life was finally working. That I had set things up beautifully. But her death changed everything.

My priorities became meaningless at the moment of her last breath. Nothing prepared me for her death, not even losing Doug six years earlier. When you actually watch someone you love die, the memory never leaves you. I was no longer just me, but became a new me, consumed by the story of my mother dying in my arms. Being present during her last moments; observing, feeling, smelling, hearing her death gurgle, transformed my life forever.

My mother's death felt like the ultimate in sharing but also was her ultimate form of rejection. Until that moment, I never comprehended how much I relied on her praise and even her envy until it was too late. Despite our difficulties, no one loved me like my mother. No one relished my stories like my mother. Now I was forced to face my life being truly

independent, all grown up and alone with no one to hear me or care. Except for my mother's ghost, with whom I often spoke.

Eventually, I stopped thinking about her every day. Then a memory would jolt me awake, invading my sleep even years later. My emotions would be as vivid as though she died again in that moment of remembering.

AFTER I LEFT home at eighteen, every time I even thought about visiting my parents, I could feel the tension mounting the closer I got to their home. I expected my father to start a fight and he rarely let me down.

He didn't dare call me names. I was seventeen the last time that happened and I had slapped him hard across the face. Then ran like hell, hiding out at a girlfriend's for two days. He never called me a slut again. My mother would beg me to try harder to get along with him. Maybe she could keep forgiving him but I couldn't, not even to make her happy.

I rarely came home but it was Christmas and I needed to be with Jeff and my mother. It was snowing lightly when I pulled into my parents' driveway. I climbed the bright red front steps. I remember when Mom painted them. I thought I'd die of embarrassment when my friends saw the vivid color. But over the years, I'd grown to appreciate that she had done something outrageous. I smiled at the memory of my older

brother, Doug taking me up in an airplane for my ninth birthday. We were able to see our house easily from the sky thanks to the color of those stairs.

THANK GOD THE hospital released Mom in time for Christmas. I had visited her a few days earlier. When I entered her ward, she announced with both arms fully extended, "This is my daughter." Then scanned her audience in the three other beds.

The collective gasp was audible as the other women in the ward turned towards me. What on earth had she been telling them? "Mom," my tone was reproachful but the truth was, I loved it.

With effort, she pushed herself to the edge of the bed and tottered to her feet. She pointed towards her overnight bag. "Let's go home, Dear." Her innocent demeanor hindered the smile at the corners of her lips. I knew she'd been at it again, bragging about me to any ear bent in her direction.

I remember when I was hired for a few minuscule, modeling jobs and my photo appeared in a Reader's Digest ad. I found twenty copies of the magazine beside her chair in the living room. A torn scrap of paper marked the page. I imagined she had sent a copy to every relative. She told me how she stood in line at the grocery store when the magazine was published and flipped through it until she found my picture, then showed it to the woman in front of her in line. "That's my daughter." The woman took the magazine and

gave it to the next woman in line, saying, "That's this woman's daughter." The ad was passed through several shoppers up to the cashier who stopped work to admire it and smile at my mother.

It didn't matter to Mom that the caption read 'An Aspiring Size Eight'. I remember struggling to get into shape, running, lifting weights, measuring the calories in everything I ate, imagining I would be featured as the 'after' model, only to discover that I was the 'before image'. 'An aspiring size eight'! I gave up on modeling.

Every time I came to visit her, I knew as soon as I left, my mother would pick up her phone and relay news of my visit to each of her sisters. She never talked about her own life but described every detail of mine. About every new man. What he did. Where we'd been on a date. What I wore. Or she would describe a trip I had just returned from or where I was going next. The gifts I had brought home for her. She hoarded any tidbit I tossed her way, sort of the way a squirrel buries nuts to fuel it over a barren winter.

She lived her life through me so I livened up my stories just for her. Basking in her praise, I stood taller, like a solitary sunflower growing erect in a field of grasses. I felt beautiful,

strong and envied, thriving more from her reactions than from the actual events. My shy, sweet mother who would never quite look directly at anyone, but when she talked about me, then her face would shine, her red cheeks blushing a little redder.

In fact, it was her flushed cheeks that became increasingly redder, that brought her to the hospital a year earlier. After she fell down the back stairs, I took her to the doctor to check for a concussion. He expressed concern over the color and wanted to run tests which lead to the discovery of a hole in her heart, followed by surgery.

After open heart surgery, while she was in Intensive Care, I sat by her side, frightened as she struggled for breath with the lung support machine plunged deep into her mouth. Tubes were everywhere. Her eyes were closed. She looked frail and helpless.

That was the first time, I faced the possibility of my mother dying. Me, the control freak, was now incapable of making things better. The thought of losing her turned me into a babbling little girl praying for her mommy.

The doctor had assured me that her surgery was a total success. Now, one year later, Mom said she was only in the hospital for a checkup.

"I should talk to the doctor before we leave." I looked toward the nurses' station.

"No," she insisted, grabbing her purse and heading towards the door. "Besides, he's already left for the holidays. I want to go home. Everything's fine."

I believed her.

ON CHRISTMAS MORNING 1978, I stamped my boots clean on those bright red steps, brushed the snow off my coat, opened the door to my parents home and called out, "Ho, ho, ho, Merry Christmas."

Jeff ran to the door. He towered over me and would be sixteen on January 1st. He threw his arms around my neck, "Merry Christmas, Bab." Even though I had long ago quit smoking, my brother's nickname held firm.

Dad called out hello from the living room while my mother came out of the kitchen, wiping her hands on her apron said, "You're just in time for the Queen." I gave her a kiss on the cheek and we joined my father in front of the television. Listening to the Queen's address was a tradition from her youth which my mother insisted we continue.

After lunch, watching the lights flicker on the artificial tree, I sat at her feet in front of the fireplace. Our stockings lay

emptied on the floor beside me – nuts, candy, a Mandarin orange. There was always a Mandarin orange.

"Here's one of those chocolate, cream-filled bells you like so much, Mom." I held one out to her.

"No thanks, Margie." She tugged at a few loose threads on her sleeve, then reached for the sewing basket and pulled out a small pair of scissors. "I intend to wear my favorite dress on New Year's Eve. Haven't gotten into it for years."

"You look great," I commented. After her heart surgery, Mom went on a diet and exercise binge. Other than her flushed complexion, she did look good.

Dad sat in his corner of the couch across the room. His unshaven whiskers formed a rough gray beard around his chin. Thinning slate hair had an orange tinge from the Grecian Formula and was still slicked back by Brylcreem. He was wearing old work pants stained a multitude of oil colors and a red, flannel lumberman's shirt. On the small side table sat his Captain Morgan rum and Diet Coke. Rum was a sailor's drink, he had proudly told me over the years. The cola was sugarless because he was diabetic. A full ashtray kept his drink company.

A few books lay by his feet, one was the copy of "The Egyptian" I had returned on my last visit. He noticed me glance at the book and said, "I have another book for you if you liked that one." He reached behind the couch, "Ah, here it is, The Robe. It's about the Roman soldier who kept Jesus'

robe after he was crucified and it transformed his life. I think you'll like it. A real classic."

"Thanks, Dad." I had become a serious reader, snubbing cheap pocket books for the classics. I was proud of not owning a television set and chose instead to play Mozart and read in the evenings. My father had a great library of old books.

As I reached for the book, I admired the painting of my mother, which hung above the fireplace. It was the largest painting Dad had done to my knowledge, an almost life size picture of my mother. They had been to the opera and he had painted it late at night after they arrived home. It was obviously done in happier times. Mom looked glamorous in her long gown and dangling crystal earrings. There was a softness to her face. She posed sitting at the baby grand piano her parents had given her.

The living room and dining room were divided by an archway. It used to be a simple door but one night Dad decided to knock out the wall and make a large opening. He was probably drunk at the time.

Dad must have read my mind when he followed my gaze towards Mom's piano where it filled most of the dining room. "Play some carols, Elaine." He stood, "We'll have a sing-a-long."

"Not now, I'm tired." Mom said.

"Come on. It'll be fun," he pushed.

"I don't feel like it."

I couldn't stop myself from interfering, "Leave her alone."

"You never feel like it anymore," Dad's voice was sad as he sat back down.

It's true. She seldom played these days. When I was little, we ordered Chinese food every Sunday and Mom would sit smiling at her piano. Dad made us sing Cole Porter and George Gershwin songs from the forties. At five, I knew the words to all of Rosemary Clooney's songs. "Thanks for the Memories" was my favourite. Dad got mad if Mom didn't keep up with his singing. These evenings often ended in her crying, so she eventually quit playing altogether.

Dad's clapping jarred me. He clapped three times, "Coffee, Elaine." He smiled at her.

Mom automatically stood. Like his bloody servant. I couldn't believe it! She may have even smiled back.

"Mom!" I held my hand out towards her imploring her to sit back down.

"It's okay, Margie. I feel like coffee too," she said and headed for the kitchen.

Glaring at my father, "She just got out of the hospital for Christ's sake." Pointing at her chair, "Sit down. I'll make it." My younger brother, Jeff looked up from his place sprawled out on the floor beside the tree, rolled his eyes with

an, 'oh, no, here-we-go-again' look and went back to sorting his hockey cards.

I stood between the refrigerator and stove where the metal table held the coffee, sugar and kettle. The surface was dirty with old coffee stains where the spoon was constantly left after stirring.

I wished she'd stand up to him. Or leave. We could sell the house and rent an apartment, live there with my brother. Well, that will never happen. Divorce was not an option in our family. She would have rather put up with the bullshit than be alone. I would leave any man who dared clap his hands at me.

I washed the spoon under the tap, wiped down the surface and picked up the cups.

"Where is everyone?" I asked when I returned to the living room and handed my mother her coffee.

Mom held her cup with both hands and inhaled the aroma before looking up and answering, "Your father is lying down in the upstairs bedroom and Jeff went downstairs to put together the stereo you gave him. That was so generous of you. Are you sure you can afford it, Dear?" my mother asked.

"Of course. He really wanted one. Music is pretty important at his age. It was for me when I was a teenager. Hard to believe he'll be sixteen next week." My heart skipped a beat remembering my sixteenth year. I sipped my Dad's coffee then added a shot of his rum.

“Actually, I think I’ll lie down for a bit also,” Mom said. “Don’t look so upset,” she patted my arm. “I’m fine. Just a little tired.”

While they napped, I sat on the front window ledge watching the snowfall. The birds were enjoying their Christmas dinner in the feeder Dad set up for them. Last summer’s flowers were hidden beneath the snow but I remembered where they slept. My father’s garden held magic even in winter.

A flash of red, as a Cardinal swooped down to grab the birdseed. I closed my eyes, the winter sun warmed me through the glass. I sat on the ledge built over the radiator and opened the window allowing the crisp air to cool my body. The hair in my nose stiffened and my breath became smoky but it felt good as I inhaled the fresh air deep into my lungs. The house felt peaceful, a rare occurrence. I turned the radio to soft carol music and began to gather up the wrapping paper and sort the gifts. As I folded the brown suit I had given Mom, I thought of how good it would look on her new slim body. The women in our family have always struggled with their weight.

Dad loved to tell the story of his first dinner at my grandmother’s. Every Friday night, Mom and her six siblings invited a friend to dinner. The servings of roast beef were paper thin, British style. After three helpings with everyone watching and waiting for him to finish, my father said he didn’t dare ask for more even though he was still hungry, so he

put down his fork and knife and thanked his future mother-in-law for a wonderful meal. Mom and her sisters cleared the table and Dad was asked to wait, in the parlor, with the other guests. Bored, he wandered into the kitchen to see what was keeping them. He found the sisters stuffing the leftovers into their mouths with great gusto.

I felt the usual anger rise as I recalled Dad's pleasure in telling that story. He acted as though it explained why he thought Mom was fat. If he had built her confidence rather than criticized her so much, perhaps she would have taken better care of herself.

A few envelopes lay on the floor beside Mom's chair and as I picked them up to place them on the mantle, I sighed, both amused and annoyed at how Mom would never sign our names on the front of an envelope so she could use them again. One of her many attempts at frugality.

She also used to collect Lucky Green Stamps. How I hated those things! All my gifts when I was young came from the Lucky Green Stamps catalogue. Mom would give me the catalogue to mark what I wanted. She would then buy only the products that gave the most green stamps. I cringed at the memory, ashamed. I used to yell that I didn't want Lucky Green Stamp gifts and would throw the catalogue at her. She would physically shrink away from me, her face crumbling. I hated her for settling for a man, who didn't make enough

money to buy real gifts from a real store the way her sisters did.

Another method she used to stretch her meager budget was to send away manufacturers coupons with the label ripped off various products. Growing up, it was a guessing game in our house opening unlabeled tins and hoping it really contained what we wanted. Mostly it was tinned peas. I can't stand them to this day.

The manufacturer would send a quarter for trying their product. Back in the 50's, 25 cents was admission to a movie. Only one coupon was allowed per customer so she would have the coins mailed to all my cousins. They certainly didn't need the money but my girlfriends and I liked receiving the envelope in the mail, feeling the coin inside. Even so, I was bloody embarrassed by it.

The first few bars sounded on the radio and I immediately felt my body stiffen in response, as it always did when I heard the words of The First Noel. I allowed my thoughts to drift imagining lifestyles for my daughter. Was she being spoiled this Christmas? She would be twelve. Had she started her period? Where was she? Could she feel me missing her? A cascade of tears welled and my heart tightened as I contemplated the life my Noel was living without me. The same questions tormented me every year. I knew the pain would surface off and on until her birthday in February. By then I would be cried out. I leaned against the wall for support and

hugged myself. Closing my eyes, I allowed the usual emotions to wash over me. The song ended with a loud Boxing Day advertisement. Releasing a deep sigh, I shook my head, shrugged my shoulders, turned off the radio and went to check on my mother.

I CRACKED OPEN her bedroom door to see how she was doing. She opened her eyes and smiled, patting the bed for me to sit with her. I leaned and kissed her cheek, inhaling Chanel #5. It was the standard Christmas gift Dad gave to us every year. I used to resent his lack of imagination but have grown to be very sentimental about that traditional perfume. I brushed her hair lightly away from her forehead as she used to do when I was a child and had awoken from a bad dream. I had found it extremely comforting and hoped she did as well.

The room had the same old tired décor as in my youth, never having been updated. Pink wallpaper with faded roses, veneer furniture from their first apartment in the forties. These were not antiques but cheap imitations.

Mom lay under the bedspread that she had crocheted with her mother back when she was a young bride. She was so proud of her handiwork. It took a whole year but helped her pass the time while Dad was overseas during World War II. She and Doug lived with our grandmother during the war. Doug had become close to our grandmother and never fully

adjusted to living with Dad when the war ended. As a teenager, he would bicycle the fifteen miles to 191 most weekends.

Mom spoke about Doug that Christmas morning. We rarely talked about my brother. As she lay in her bed, she told me that she had lost him years before he actually died. After he left for university, he rarely came home. Perhaps she found him again that day. Perhaps he was waiting for her on the other side of life. I hope so.

"Take care of your father for me, will you?" she said suddenly, grasping my hand tightly.

"Of course, "I answered, thinking she meant just for today. I sensed no urgency. I simply thought she meant to take care of Dad because Christmas was always sad for my father. His mother died a few days before Christmas in 1940 when he was a bachelor of thirty-one. In 1943, as the story went, my father asked his dad what he wanted to do for Christmas?

'To spend it with your mother,' my grandfather had answered.

'No, I need you here with me,' my father replied.

'Okay, I'll make you a deal,' my grandfather reportedly said, 'I'll have lunch with you and dinner with your mother.' He died on Christmas afternoon.

My father was miserable every Christmas. He drank more than usual and emotionally repeated the story in a slurred voice each year. I never felt connected to his sadness since I hadn't known his parents. Instead, I resented the story

because it ruined our holiday. I never wanted to be reminded of his story. And now I have my own.

"I don't need to ask you to take care of Jeff. You always have." My mother continued. "Honey, go get my purse," she pointed to the dresser.

I walked over and brought it to her. She took out a check which was made payable to her and endorsed it over to me. "Here, go get yourself something special."

I was shocked. It was an unusual gesture. "Mom, I already have my present from you."

"That's from your father and me. This is special, just between us."

I should have known then that something was terribly wrong. Mom had never given me a gift separate from my father. Without question, I took the check. Later, I used the money to buy a new gold chain with it to hold the locket my grandmother had given Mom when she graduated from the University of Toronto. The original chain was severely damaged. I wore that locket and chain every day, and whenever I felt the need to be close to the women who had loved me, I would hold the gold, feel its history and quietly pray for my mother's and grandmother's guidance.

"Thanks, Mom. Now go to sleep. I'm concerned. I'm going to call the hospital and ask if I should take you back."

"No! Don't do that." She sat up in bed, her floral nightie slipping off her shoulder. Adjusting it, she continued, "I'm okay. Really. Just tired. I don't want to go back."

"If the hospital agrees, okay. Rest for now and I'll let you know what they say." After a quick hug, too quick for all eternity, I closed her door.

The nurse who answered the phone, wouldn't take responsibility. 'Call her doctor,' she advised. I got his answering service and left a message.

It was most likely the doctor calling back later that afternoon that woke Mom. I didn't hear the phone from the basement. None of us did. Mom ran from the bedroom to answer but got there too late. Was it that jarring run that provoked her heart attack? If I had heard the phone would things have turned out differently?

Mom found us in the basement. My cousin, Chuck had come over and was showing my brother and I a home video of his last trip to Vancouver. Mom settled on the old couch to watch with us. The final scene was of the sunset over English Bay. The sky burst into color as it set behind the mountains. I never see that scene without thinking of my mother. Since I've moved to Vancouver, I often go and watch the sunset whenever I feel the need to be close to her. It has come to represent her saying good night to me.

When the film ended, we all sighed with the beauty of it. Mom turned to me. She held out her arms. Everything became

still as if there was no one else in the room. Just her across the room with her arms open wide. I pushed up from my chair. I held my arms out too, moving slowly as if in slow motion. She kept my gaze. Nothing else existed. Just her arms waiting for me, her face full of love, beaming, smiling at me. I felt her arms around me. The embrace, not knowing where she ended and I began.

Holding her, I felt her gasp. She died in my arms.

It took a moment before I realized what had happened. Still encompassed by her, I wanted to stay in that moment of eternal love forever. My cousin was yelling. With the sound of her death gurgle, I pulled away and looked at her motionless face and then felt her arms drop from around me. I screamed, "No!" I yelled at Jeff to call an ambulance. "Please help." My cousin pushed me aside and began mouth-to-mouth resuscitation. I sat on the floor at her feet and screamed. "No, no, no!"

I watched as my cousin leaned over her. Feeling helpless, feeling ownership, "She's my Mother, let me do it." Switching places, my mouth on hers, I tried desperately to breathe life back into her. I didn't know what I was doing. My cousin stood beside me giving instructions. I could hear my brother screaming into the phone for an ambulance. Still, I clung to my mother as she lay lifeless beside me. I kissed her lips, "Please, Mommy, please, Mommy."

Twenty minutes must have pasted before the ambulance arrived. The medics rushed into the room and pushed me aside. Helpless, I watched as they applied shock volts to resuscitate her heart. "Please let her be okay. Is she okay?" They didn't answer. They ignored me. "Please, Mommy. I need you. Please SOMEBODY DO SOMETHING!" The medics moved her to a stretcher and started towards the door. I followed as closely as they would allow. "Jeff, tell Dad," I yelled. He was still asleep upstairs.

"No, Jeff, go with your sister to the hospital. I'll tell your father," my cousin ordered. So brave of him. He took charge. His own mother, my mother's sister Margaret, died on Christmas Day in 1969. How many are to die on Christmas Day in this family?

At the hospital, the nurse walked into the waiting room. "I'm sorry," she said. There was no need to say anything else. I knew.

"Someone needs to identify the body."

"Why? We came in with her."

"She died outside the hospital. It's routine. You'll also have to file a police report. They're waiting to take your statement."

Jeff offered to go for me. I couldn't let him. He was still a kid, just turning sixteen the following week.

THERE MUST BE such a thing as a soul because the body feels so different in death. I removed her rings. She was already cold and her skin leathery.

I touched my own hands and felt her life in me. It was as though I had just now been ripped from her womb. Shocked, I remember thinking, 'So this is what it feels like to lose your mother.' The pain is so immense. So forever. It was like falling into an open pit, bottomless, falling, falling, with no end.

As we reached home, the snow had started again. Jeff and I held each other up as we slid our way towards the house. I could see Dad in his flannelette robe standing hopefully at the window. He looked old. Frail. It's the first time I realized how he had aged. No longer the frightening giant of my youth. At seventy-one, he had actually shrunk and I hadn't noticed.

Now I had to deliver this news. Once again, I would be a messenger of death.

The bells on the Christmas wreath jingled as I pushed open the front door. Dad's eyes questioned me with a stunned look that couldn't hide his panic. Eyes expecting the worst, yet pleading for some hope.

"She's dead, Daddy," was all I could say, my arms limp at my side. Confused, his face contorted. Then, his pain. I held him as he cried, his grief added to mine. We found a common ground in our sorrow. My anger towards him forgotten as we mourned together.

Jeff stood and watched us, then turned and left for his job at the bingo hall where he called out the numbers for elderly women. We tried to convince him not to go but there was nothing Father nor I could say to stop him. He didn't tell anyone about the tragic events of his day.

Dad and I polished off a bottle of Captain Morgan.

A FEW DAYS later, I searched her personal articles. I found little of value. Only cheap trinkets. Nothing I could wear and say proudly, 'This belonged to my mother.' Mostly, she had costume jewelry from my father, bought on a shopping spree after a large printing job, to match a new dress. Some souvenirs I brought her from various parts of the world: a gold plated seashell necklace from Hawaii, Capiz shell earrings from Manila, jade beads from Japan, probably fake and a Canadian quarter necklace from San Francisco which had the background carved out so that the deer stood encircled by the coin on a silver plated chain. There were no diamonds, only her gold locket which I clutched lovingly, remembering our last moments together. I held it against my cheek. I wanted my mother to have had jewels, real valuables, to be spoiled, to be loved, to be held in esteem.

I kept her brush. It became sacred. I noticed my reflection in her oval mirror. I looked so much like grandmother and mother with our full moon-shaped faces, straight blonde hair, blue/green eyes under arched eyebrows.

But our natures weren't at all alike. My eyes held a strength and determination I didn't see in my ancestors. I think it came from a confidence I suspect they didn't feel. The confidence of survival.

I found one drawer stuffed with travel brochures and a note attached which read, "Margie says we can fly anywhere American Airlines goes for free and get cheap passes on 27 airlines." My face fell as I read her note and thought about how much we both looked forward to taking trips together now that I worked for the airlines. I was curious to see what countries attracted my mother. I flipped through brochures which focused on Europe. Paris and Rome seemed the highest on her list. I would always regret that she never got to see those cities.

Jeff opened the door. "Café au lait?" he said in a fake French accent as he held out a cup of coffee. I took the cup, breathing in the rich aroma while observing my brother. Any semblance of childhood had disappeared on Christmas day. His blue eyes were solemn but revealed nothing. He kissed the top of my head then turned to leave. I grabbed his hand. It smelled of resin from the model plane he had been building. I held his hand against my cheek for a moment, then released him. My eyes lingered on the closed door. My familiar yearning for a child surfaced. I vowed I would have a baby when I was ready, man or no man. The father would be bright, ambitious, musical, artsy, interested in travel and other

cultures. A lot like Doug. Boys, I would only give birth to boys. I had no doubt my life would play out exactly as I orchestrated it.

I opened another dresser drawer and that's when I found her note. I don't know what compelled me to go through her belongings so soon, before she was even buried. What would I have done if I found it long afterwards?

The note simply said, 'Please make sure I am really dead. I've read that people have been buried when they are only in a coma.' When did she write such a thing? Last year, before the heart surgery? Or more recently?

Common sense told me that once she was embalmed, it would be impossible for her to be alive, still I went to the phone, called the funeral home and asked to have her casket opened when I arrived.

I slipped quickly through the lobby into the small room containing my mother's body. Her coffin was raised on a platform, the lid was already raised. Organ music was playing softly. White poinsettias were in abundance, with sympathy cards tucked between the blossoms.

I moved beside the coffin. I felt the skin on her hand. It was cold and tough like leather, no longer supple or soft. I held my hand below her nose. I leaned my ear as close to her heart as the coffin would allow and listened quietly. Yes, she was dead. There was no mistaking it. How terrified she must have been to write that note. Who did she think would find it?

Would Dad have come to the funeral home? Why hadn't she confided her fears instead of pretending she was fine?

'Don't discuss anything painful,' our family motto was honored to the bitter end.

Why didn't you tell me, Mommy? You could have talked to me. I cared. I would have done something. I should have made you go to the doctor. If only you'd been honest. Why didn't you let me take you to the hospital?

If only... **tears choked off the words. Could the staff at the hospital have saved her if she had the attack there. If only they had told me to bring her back instead of calling the doctor. He called on Boxing Day to say he was sorry. Too bloody late, I told him, she's dead.**

Why can't we ever talk in this family?

I sat beside her coffin for another half hour, my questions unanswered then I kissed her lifeless cheek, and placed a solitary white rose on her chest and walked away.

THE CHRISTMAS TREE disappeared. I don't remember who removed it. I took a leave of absence from my reservations job at American Airlines, gave notice at my apartment and moved into the spare bedroom upstairs. Jeff had taken over the basement room after I moved out ten years earlier.

Dad and I sat up late together every night, drinking rum and smoking cigarettes. I would come into the room and

catch him staring at Mom's portrait. He would ramble on, recalling his memories of their time together as though it had been a marriage made in heaven. Every week, my father bought a solitary red rose from the local florist and placed beside his painting of her. A lot of good his romanticism did her now. With my thoughts hidden, I would travel the landscape of my own version of things.

We celebrated Jeff's sixteenth birthday on New Year's day. When the restaurant hostess sat us at our table, it was set for four. I froze. I held out my hand, palm up, "There are only three of us. Please take one away."

Jeff shook my arm, "Let's just go home." But, Dad and I were determined.

The dining room overlooked the gardens, which extended back to the Scarborough Bluffs. The Guild Inn had presided over all of my mother's family celebrations going back to my great-grandmother's era. The tradition died on my brother's sixteenth birthday. We never went back.

We sat, absent eyed, food untouched, gifts discarded on the floor. It was a day to be acknowledged and endured. The poor waitress must have been stunned when she asked how things were and my father burst into tears. I kept thinking of Mom wearing her dress on New Year's. We had buried her in it and I tried desperately to stop thinking of her cold body rotting underground.

Jeff disappeared to the refuge of his bingo hall soon after we got home. His sixteenth year, was destined to be as miserable as mine had been.

I was tormented by memories of my mother's last breath and would sit up in bed, crying. Every night, Jeff slept beside me on a mattress placed on the floor. *Did I kill her? I should have let my cousin do the mouth-to-mouth. I should demanded she go to the hospital.* Jeff would wake up and sit on my bed, holding my hand. The more my emotions poured out, the more my brother concealed his own feelings. Did he think he needed to be strong for my father and me? I wanted to help him but he wouldn't let me and I was unable to stop my own sorrow from erupting constantly.

CHAPTER 16

I HAD PROMISED my mother I'd take care of my father and I did. I made sure he and Jeff ate fresh vegetables. I cooked and cleaned.

Dad clapped for coffee only once. Had he really expected me to jump up the way she had? Without moving, I told him, "You raised me to be a lady, you'll treat me like a lady. And," I glared at him, "I would love a coffee while you're up." Our eyes connected. There wasn't a sound as we both held our breath waiting for the other to react.

Poor Jeff couldn't stand the tension and jumped up, "I feel like a coffee. I'll get it."

My father never clapped at me again.

AFTER THREE WEEKS, I went back to work but the following spring, I took another leave. This time for six months. I traveled to Mexico, the Caribbean, Japan, Thailand, Burma, Hong Kong, England, Turkey, Cyprus, Egypt, Argentina, Peru and Brazil. I visited Henry in the Philippines.

It felt good visiting on my own without him paying my way. That year, I used more free passes than anyone, ever, in the history of American Airlines.

Still every time I closed my eyes, I relived Christmas day and questioned why Mom died so young? Her at 59 and Doug at 28. I couldn't sleep for a solid year. Chuck, the cousin who was with us the day mom died, suggested I attend a self - help seminar he had taken. EST was controversial at the time.

Considered a cult by some, it was a two weekend seminar based on a compilation of several New Age beliefs. It emphasized integrity, accountability and taking responsibility for how you experienced events in your life. One exercise involved standing silently at the front of the room being observed by a few hundred people. When it was my turn to observe the people on the stage, I was amazed to see people shake or cry, fearful of my observation of them. All these years, I thought everyone gossiped about me and here they were worried about themselves!

I learned to be an observer of my own emotional reactions rather than reacting. Although I remained true to the family motto of secrecy at all costs and was never able to discuss the pain of giving up my daughter for adoption, I came to realize that everyone, including my father, was concerned with their own issues, not mine and doing the best they could with their own life circumstances.

The exercises not only helped to stop my nightmares but also healed my relationship with my father. After the seminar, I started to ask Dad questions about his life. I would observe myself reacting to him and saw how I had allowed him to upset me. Now instead of concentrating on how he had been an imperfect husband and father, I set out to discover who was this man, my father? I noticed how he could push my buttons. Once I stopped reacting and allowed him to say what he needed to say, he stopped baiting me.

It's difficult to imagine how anything positive could result from an experience as painful as my mother's death but it did. I realized that if my father had died before my mother, I would never have gotten to know and love him as I did. We started having real conversations and enjoyed a loving relationship for the rest of his life. And because I could never again celebrate Christmas, my mother's last gift to me was the freedom to marry a Jew.

BOOK TWO

VANCOUVER 1991

DAVID CAME INTO the kitchen and grabbed me by the hand, pulling me close. We danced to the radio playing, Bryan Adams, 'Everything I do, I do it for you'. Dropping the potato I was peeling, I let him swing me around. God, I was happy.

I met my husband at a dance, five days after I moved to Vancouver to start my career as a stockbroker. Actually, he picked me up in a bar but I think a dance sounds so much nicer. At the end of the evening, I handed him my new business card. "Call me sometime. I'd love to go dancing with you again." He became my first client.

David was good for business, promoting me to other lawyers whenever he could. Usually he told them, "She made me a small fortune." He would pause for effect then add, "I used to have a large fortune." Laughing boisterously, he would hug me and wink. He gave me advice on problems at work. His protective concern and encouragement reminded me of my brother, Doug. I felt safe.

He was a Jew with a Mediterranean look, a strong Roman nose and thick glasses. Divorced with two kids, an ex-wife with

whom he was on good terms and a strong bond with his parents who believed he should only marry within his faith. He wanted me to convert. When asked, I suddenly became attached to a God I had lost interest in years earlier.

My family barely spoke while his never stopped talking.

So different from my exotic travels, David went to the same hotel in Maui for the same two weeks every year, playing tennis and golf with the same friends.

He was an athlete, scrawny and tall, moving through a room like a human vibrator with no off-switch. He was country club, whereas I was a loner whose recreation involved reading the financial pages at the beach.

I chatted with parking attendants. Strangers felt comfortable telling me their life stories. With David, if the conversation wasn't political enough or intelligent enough, it didn't happen. He hated pretense, but often slipped details of his accomplishments into the conversation.

My investment instructor described me as someone who 'would take on bulls' while David once confessed that sometimes he was not confident about his success. He said he felt as though he was fooling everyone. But when he dressed in his robes and stepped into the courtroom, he transformed into Clarence Darrow. He used his humility as his strength, pretending to be incompetent, while rattling off mathematical calculations on a case for hours without glancing at a single note. Watching him perform in court, I beamed with pride.

His high school photos and thick glasses spelled: Nerd. We would never have acknowledged each other back in the sixties.

I was clear that eventually I wanted babies. He had two daughters and didn't want more children.

Although it appeared we had nothing in common, one evening, with my head lowered in shame, I confided my secret past. He brushed my hair behind my ear and gently lifted my face towards him - an unconscious move on his part, but it touched an essential place deep within me. Then he wept. This bonded me to him in a way laughter never could.

Over the years, I became attached to his daughters. Yael was four when we first met. She had an impish smile and would crawl into my lap like a Lhasa Apso. I thought her turned up nose, freckles and blue eyes made her resemble a child David and I might have had together. People often mistook me for her mother. I liked that.

Shiera was a carbon copy of her father – dark, Mediterranean skin, curly black hair, a strong Semitic nose. Hers was an exotic look and once people met Shiera, they rarely forgot her. She was tall when I met her at seven and by thirteen, she towered over me. It was difficult to think of her as a child. David said she was born looking grown up. There was nothing passive about Shiera. She was powerful and her presence was felt the minute she entered a room. Her height and strong voice commanded an audience. We often clashed.

CHAPTER 2

I WISH I could find that boy so I could thank him. It was Easter Sunday, 1988, one of those glorious spring days in Vancouver when everyone forgets that it rained all winter and enjoys the lushness of the earth.

I had the top down on my convertible and was on my way to a friends for dinner. As I pulled into the Esso station at Garden City and Westminster Highway, the attendant came to my car and altered everything, unknowingly, with his words.

"Great day, eh?" I agreed wholeheartedly. "Beautiful car." He started to wash my windshield. "Le Baron, isn't it?"

"Yes," I answered him.

"What year?" he asked.

"83," I told him.

"Oh, it doesn't look five years old. You take good care of it. Must have your son polishing it every weekend."

"No. I don't have a son," I replied.

"Your daughter then," he said.

"No, I don't have a daughter either."

"Well, your husband?"

Starting to get upset, I told him curtly, "I don't have a husband."

“A brother?” he quizzed me as he replaced the hose.

“Not here,” I answered. Jeff used to visit every summer, but that ended when he began a career as a stock broker in Toronto. No chance of him moving here now.

“Well, you gotta have a boyfriend?”

“I’m single.” I answered, growing visibly upset. He just wouldn’t let up. It wasn’t his business that David and I had been dating for eight years without any long term commitments.

“Gee, I’m sorry.” He took my credit card and went inside to process it.

Signing the slip, I handed it back to him. “Happy Easter,” he smiled.

“Yeah.” I pulled away so he couldn’t see the tears when they burst through my resolve. The realization that I didn’t want to be alone anymore hit me hard. I drove straight to David’s apartment. Once I made up my mind, the poor guy didn’t have a chance. We were married a few months later.

CHAPTER 3

NOW DANCING IN his arms, I felt exhilarated. This time I was certain.

I thought about the card I'd bought for his birthday the following weekend. It read, 'Happy Birthday, Daddy, love from Samuel Douglas.' That was the name we had chosen for our son when I would finally get pregnant. Samuel after David's late grandfather and Douglas after my brother. In the Jewish tradition, family names could only be used if the relative was deceased.

The card would be my way of breaking the news. My period was several weeks late and I could feel our baby inside me. But I forced myself to wait for David's birthday.

"I wish I could crawl inside you," I smiled.

David kissed my forehead, pulled me closer and swept me off my feet all over again.

When the song ended, I threw my arms around him. "I'm going to hang on to your neck all day. You'll just have to take me to court with you cuz I won't let go."

"What'll I tell the judge?"

“I’ll tell him, excuse me, your Honor, but I’m so in love with my husband that I couldn’t let go. Please ignore me and go on with the proceedings.”

CHAPTER 4

IT WOULD HAVE been romantic except my period started the next day. I looked at the words Samuel Douglas once more before I opened the garbage pail and tossed out the card. My doctor explained that sometimes a woman could will herself into the symptoms of pregnancy. Oh well, next month for sure.

I timed my cycles carefully to be certain I was ovulating. I took my temperature. I elevated my legs up after sex to help the little fellows reach their destination. I visualized my fertilized eggs. I pictured new life forming inside me. I talked to Samuel Douglas by name. When I wrote down my goals, my baby boy was always at the top of my list. Knowing I had friends in heaven, I got down on my knees, held my mother's locket and prayed.

In fact, I prayed to anyone who might listen. I tried them all – Mom, Dad, my grandmother, Doug. Even St. Jude, the Patron Saint of Hopeless Cases. I was certainly a hopeless case. To stay optimistic, I'd sing uplifting songs and repeat Buddhist chants.

When will they get home? It's late and they should be here by now. I feel wet from sweating. God, it's hot. That Toronto heat where

nothing cools you off. Those nights when the fan blows the sultry night air, thick with humidity, around the room. Nothing helps cool you and you sleep naked under a single cotton sheet.

The kitchen is a mess. The same linoleum for forty years which needs replacing but it won't happen, since there's no money. Looking out the window, I see the branches of the crab apple tree thick with white blossoms drift down like snow.

Where are they? I'm worried. I don't like being here alone. The tea has gone cold. Then I noticed the old gray Hillman parked in the driveway. Wait. What is going on? My parents haven't driven a Hillman since the fifties. Something's wrong.

MY EYES OPEN. It took a minute to realize where I was. David continued his gentle snore. Oh God, not again. Why do I keep dreaming they're alive? Tears, silently so as not to wake David, glide down my face into my ears and hair. I wait for dawn to peek through the crack in the curtains.

It's always the same. I'm waiting at the house for them to return. For Mom, really but she's late. At first I imagine she is out enjoying herself with a lover and I'm happy for her. But it grows late and still she hasn't returned. I start to worry. Waiting and waiting, only to sit up in bed startled when I realize it was another dream. My mother is dead.

Lately Doug has been in the dreams also. I hear him playing 'Moon River' on the piano and I rush to his side. The

dreams are so real I'm forced to mourn them all over again when I wake up.

David appears so peaceful. He doesn't share my pain. He has his daughters and family while I long for mine.

As I lay there in the early morning, my heart is beating fast. My entire nervous system is racing which terrifies me considering how young Doug and Mom were when they died. I take several deep breathes and try to relax by repeating a mantra but my stress has taken on a life of its own. I quietly get out of bed, dress and go for a long walk.

I FIND MY voice rising aggressively in conversations. I'm becoming angry at everything and everybody. In my head, I'm constantly trying to justify my behavior by blaming everyone else and mumbling to myself, 'he said, she said, they said.' I was becoming one of those street people who talk to themselves.

I have another recurring dream. David has left me. When I tell him, he says I should be happy with what I have. He's getting impatient with my mood swings but it never occurred to me that when I was ready to have my baby boy, I wouldn't get pregnant. After all, Mom had my brother when she was forty-five. But we've had been trying since we got married three years earlier. Now at forty-two, I'm running out of time.

FINALLY, I CONSULTED a specialist who suggested I try fertility drugs. They didn't work. In fact, they only made things worse. Each month, my body, geared up by the drugs to become pregnant. Then when I didn't, I would fall into a terrible depression. The first month, not understanding the hormonal upheaval the drugs were causing, I announced to David that I was moving to Africa to open an orphanage for mentally and physically disabled, black Pygmy children. As ridiculous as that sounded, it seemed to me the only alternative available other than suicide. Once I realized this erratic behavior was caused by the drugs, it was easier, but my unfulfilled need remained.

CHAPTER 5

THE NURSE LED me into the fertility doctor's office. He pointed to the seat in front of him and opened a file on his desk. "We have the results back from all of the tests we ran."

"Yes," I responded, waiting.

"You have a condition called Adenomyosis which in layman's terms means that the walls of your uterus are collapsing." He waited for me to respond. I couldn't speak. "One of your tubes is severely damaged. The other tube is inconclusive, but in all my years of practice, I've never seen one tube this badly damaged while the other functions properly. We could do a laparoscopy if you like but frankly I don't see much point."

"What about in vitro fertilization?" I leaned forward hopefully.

"The placenta won't be able to build up to provide the necessary nourishment for the fetus. You'd most likely miscarry. I've seldom seen in vitro take in a woman with your condition. Besides, at forty-two, you're too old to be covered by the medical plan in Canada. The cut off is thirty-eight."

"What about the States?"

"You could go to Seattle but it would cost approximately ten thousand each try and it generally takes

several attempts even without your condition. My research suggests you have at best a four percent chance of conceiving and even less of carrying a baby full term."

I felt the room close in on me. A poster of a happy mother holding her baby smiled down at me from the doctor's wall. I hadn't noticed it before. The doctor sat quietly waiting for my response. He looked so clinical. Does he understand my disappointment at his news or has he conditioned himself to not feel involved? I felt numb. Why could he make babies for everyone else and not me? It's not fair.

The heat rose in my face and my eyes started to water. I did not want to cry in his office. I stood before I broke down. "Thank you doctor." I offered him my hand. He took it and held it in both of his.

"I'm sorry. I know how you must feel." his voice soft.

Breathing deeply, holding back the tears, I nodded and fled his office. I didn't wait for the elevator, not wanting anyone to see the tears I could no longer hold back. I ran down four flights of stairs to hide in my car.

"It's not fair. It's just not fair. Oh God, I want a baby!" I screamed to the universe. Hiding in the darkness of the basement parking lot, I let the tears flow freely. "Samuel Douglas, you must be born. Please don't do this to me. I beg you. Give me this one thing. Please. Please don't do this. It

can't be true. There must be a mistake." My cheeks flushed, my throat burned and I started to heave. I couldn't catch my breath. Gasping for air, I thought, I could die right there. I slammed my fist into the dashboard. "No, no, no."

Shaking, I sat for half an hour before I could pull myself together. I drove to English Bay where I sat under a tree looking at the same sunset my mother watched on my cousin's video the day she died. I had often sat there over the past fourteen years, having conversations with her. "Please help me, Mom. I don't know what to do."

I sat hugging my knees until I finally admitted there were no miracles or magic answers and talking to my dead mother under a tree wasn't getting me anywhere. I took a deep breath, shook my shoulders. It was time to face my demons.

CHAPTER 6

I PARKED IN the circular driveway of the Tudor mansion. An elegant East Indian woman opened the door.

"Hello. I'm Doctor Singh," she said, smiling.

Tapestries adorned the walls, Persian rugs covered hardwood floors. She wore an enormous diamond on her hand. I glanced towards a floor-to-ceiling bookshelf brimming with antique leather-bound books. Psychiatry obviously paid well. Maybe I could land her as a client.

"The fertility specialist told me you specialize in women's issues," I said.

"Yes."

"I'm sure you have patients with real problems." I believed that simply by being there, I was admitting I couldn't cope.

"Why not tell me what's troubling you. Let me worry whether or not you should be here. Okay?"

Thus began my weekly meetings with Dr. Singh. I confessed how real my baby had felt and my now overwhelming despair. She was amazed I had been so confident I could get pregnant in my early forties. Yet despite what the specialist told me, I still found it difficult to believe I was sterile. Every month, I

continued to hope to become pregnant. I thought that by relaxing, not trying too hard, I would conceive.

Dr. Singh wanted to know everything. Had I sued the manufacturer of the IUD? Yes, but it seems my sterility was only worth three grand because I had switched brands. Besides no amount of money could ever make up for not having a baby.

She probed my relationship with my husband, asking about money, exploring the Cinderella Syndrome, the theory that a woman marries her prince to be taken care of forever. But I assured her that I had always taken care of myself and even though David was a successful lawyer I contributed equally to our finances.

I CHOSE THE career of stockbroker shortly after my mother died. I did it to imitate the men I admired most. My brother Doug started investing in the stock market with his photography earnings at eleven when our uncle took him under his wing. Uncle Basil was a self-made man who survived the 1929 crash – barely. He had seven children at the time and confessed to me how he wanted to commit suicide so his family could live on his insurance policy. He didn't. I kept my uncle's photograph on my desk at work, glancing at his kind, confident smile during stressful markets. I had no family counting on me, so if my uncle could survive 1929, I could survive any daily fluctuations the stock market threw at me.

If I closed my eyes, I could imagine the waves lapping against the dock pilings and the sound of my uncle's inlaid wood boat gently tapping against the buoys at his private island in the Muskokas which he bought with the earnings from his first big score in the stock market. It was The Great Gatsby, Duddy Kravitz, The Hamptons and the Adirondacks all nicely folded into his elaborate cottage. We, the poor relatives, were invited each summer.

My father dropped into my aunt and uncle's tea and crumpet world from Planet Captain Morgan. But even he was happy at my uncle's cottage paradise where he would wander off to a quiet spot, set up his easel, his Captain Morgan rum and diet Coke on a rock beside him. Our house was full of paintings of Edith Island.

Mom, in her old-fashioned bathing suit, covering as much as possible, would lie peacefully like Gatsby's Daisy in her chaise lounge. There was sense of peace at the cottage - that of another era. My parents' fights were left behind, unpacked, at home.

My aunt would tell me happy stories of how her two children who died young would visit her dreams at night. Even death wasn't final here.

During the day, my aunt and I would pick wild blueberries, enough to bake a pie. As a young girl, I played in their special house built just for little people, or we'd play cards on the huge verandah while Mom watched, sipping lemonade, with her feet dangling over the edge of the rattan love seat. In the

evening, my mother played the piano and we would sing. She appeared more comfortable in their world than in ours.

At night over bonfires with flames reflected in the lake, we would roast hot dogs and marshmallows. On Edith Island, I never got yelled at if one fell into the fire. Meals were feasts and I was allowed to pile as many slices of meat as I could fit into a bun, making sandwiches so big my lips barely fit around them. At my uncle's cottage, there was no mother crying silently in the kitchen because there wasn't enough food to serve.

It was no wonder both my brothers and I went into the investment business. All of us wanted to become Uncle Basil and not follow in our father's footsteps. There would be no romantic starving artists for us.

So no, Doctor Singh, I didn't marry my husband for a meal ticket.

NEXT, DOCTOR SINGH implied I was jealous of David's relationship with his daughters. I've never denied this. "He thinks I should just get over not having a baby and be happy with the relationship I have with my step daughters." I had this conversation on a regular basis with my husband. I would accuse him of being happy I couldn't get pregnant. I knew my sterility wasn't his fault but I was frustrated and angry.

"Tell me why it's so devastating for you?" Dr. Singh asked.

"I need a baby. All my life I dreamed of the privilege of planning, conceiving and raising a baby with a man I loved. I wanted someone to give up their seat on the bus for me. David laughs at that because I never take the bus but I would if I was pregnant just to experience it once."

I wanted to enjoy a pregnancy, not like before. In hindsight, I should have gotten pregnant years ago on my own. I thought about it many times but I was busy with my career and truly believed I could have a baby pretty much at any age I wanted. " I got so frustrated with her questions. I stood and started pacing her small den. "I yearned for my daughter. Every Christmas, every birthday. I don't know where she is. If she's happy. I don't even know if she's alive. Can you possibly imagine what that feels like?" I was screaming by now. I paused and leaned against the fireplace, then continued in a quiet voice, "She could be dead and I wouldn't even know."

Dr. Singh handed me a tissue. "Go on."

It drove me crazy how she just sat there. I had to remind myself that it wasn't Dr. Singh who forced me to give up my daughter. This wasn't her war. She was here to help me.

We talked about my mother and brother dying so young. She felt I hadn't finished mourning them. What did she think? Of course I missed them. What did she expect? That I was going to wake up one day and it would be okay that they died so young?

CHAPTER 7

AFTER SEVERAL MONTHS of weekly visits, Dr. Singh asked, "Was incest possible?"

I guess she was doing her job, but no way, Dad had never touched me sexually.

She continued to explore my past, insisting we examine my family and its dysfunctional secrecy. But even I was shocked at the memories her probing evoked.

"Tell me more about your relationship with your father," Dr. Singh asked one afternoon.

"Well, he was older than my mom. He wore dotted bow ties."

"You've told me some of the problems. Now tell me what you liked about him."

"Hmmm," I was surprised by her question. I closed my eyes and sunk deeper into her paisley love seat. I tried to think of something I liked about my father. I glanced at Dr. Singh's dark complexion and remembered, "When I was a little girl, he spoke to me about foreign places like India and Japan. I dreamed of visiting exotic countries when I grew up and I did." I smiled. "Dad did things. He ran away from home as a young boy and

joined the Navy. He traveled all over the world. I got my personality from him, that's for sure."

"I want you to close your eyes and go back to a time when you were happy with your father." I kicked off my shoes and stretched my legs out on her wooden coffee table, careful not to knock the vase of colorful spring flowers. Closing my eyes, I could picture him.

"Where are you?"

"In my parent's living room." I answered.

"How old are you?"

"Four or five. We had just bought our first T.V.."

"Okay, just relax and tell me whatever pops into your head."

"It's late and we're watching television. Mom is saying that I have to go to bed. Dad's ignoring her."

"Go on."

"I remember now, I used to fall asleep on his lap every night. I forgot about that and how nice it felt." I raised my head and pushed up with my elbows, looking across the room to the doctor sitting quietly taking notes at her desk. "I fall asleep on my husband's lap now. Interesting."

She nodded for me to continue. "Dad would read to me from Sinbad the Sailor or Arabian Nights. His words were like a magic carpet. He loved different cultures and taught me to be interested in faraway places. When David told me about some of the anti-Semitic things that happened to him, I was shocked because there was no prejudice in my home. My first boyfriend

was Japanese. The second was part Mohawk Indian. I dated a Hungarian, a Greek, Italians, a Filipino. Dad embraced them all.

Dr. Singh helped me remember things long forgotten. Memories that had been shut out came flooding back as I related stories about growing up with my father.

"He had a sense of humor, my Dad and he was a great cook. Life in the kitchen was exciting. Mom cooked the same old dishes, but Dad was exotic. He made cream puffs. He added spices no woman would consider, until it tasted right. That's why all great chefs are men, Dad would say, because they have no preconditioned ideas of what goes together. We'd go on picnics where my Dad painted in the woods while I would swim in the river or hike the hills."

"When did your father start drinking?" Dr. Singh asked.

I thought back and remembered it was after his business was destroyed during Hurricane Hazel. He rented space in the basement of an office building and it flooded, destroying his inventory of paper and damaging one of his two printing presses. He didn't have insurance and was forced to move into our garage. Mom's family loaned him money so he could start working again. "He sold out to support us kids, I guess."

"How so?"

"He was an artist. My mother's relatives didn't consider art much of a career. He tried to conform but it wasn't his nature. Mom and Dad fought constantly. Mostly about money. I begged them to stop. Dad would go off in a rage and drink alone in his shop. He didn't spend time with me anymore. I thought it was my

fault. Mom watered down his booze and cursed him under her breathe."

"You heard her?"

"All the time. She would stand in the kitchen and empty half of a new bottle of rum into the old one and fill both up with water, repeating she hated him over and over."

Dr. Singh leaned forward, "Do you think this may have influenced your feelings towards him?"

"I guess." It must have been impossible for Dad with her family belittling him. I wondered, *Did you really teach me to hate him, Mom? Were you jealous of our closeness? Did you ruin it between us?*

I closed my eyes, sinking into the couch, "One day, I remember the police were there." I stopped, surprised at the thought and wondering where it came from.

"Go on. Don't stop now."

"I don't know if I want to."

"It's okay. Tell me what you see."

I clenched a pillow, "The police were there. I had just come home from school. There was an ambulance. My Dad was in the police car with lights flashing. A few neighbours were standing around watching. My mother, clutching her flowered apron, was standing beside an officer answering questions. I was scared. Doug was pulling me towards the house. I didn't want to go. I wanted to know what's going on. Why is my Daddy in the police car? Has he done something wrong? Doug tightened his grip on my arm when I try to run to my father. Dad's head was

down. He wouldn't look at me. I shouted, "What's wrong with my Daddy? Why won't you tell me what's happening?" Dr. Singh stood with a tissue and placed her arm on my shoulder. I hadn't realized I was crying.

I glanced towards Dr. Singh, "An ambulance came and they made me go inside, but I heard them. Someone whispered suicide." I stopped choking on my words. I gasped for air.

"Don't stop," Dr. Singh urged in an excited voice, "Your father tried to commit suicide?"

I can see it. I had forgotten.

"He drank chemicals from his printing shop." It was another bloody family secret.

"How old were you?"

"Five or six, I think." I looked up at Dr. Singh. "God, we covered it up like everything else. That's when he started to drink, after Hurricane Hazel."

I could see his face in the police car. He was sort of grayish and even though I didn't realize it at the time, he appeared defeated, his shoulders slumped. He wouldn't look at me even though I was screaming and trying to break loose of Doug's grip. Mom ordered my brother to get me out of there." I felt my whole body shake with the memory.

I looked into Dr. Singh's sympathetic eyes, "He was never the same. Not the feisty fighter I had known. He sank into a depression and wouldn't play with me anymore. I thought he didn't love me."

Jesus, did this really happen? Or was I making it all up? It felt real, but I couldn't imagine I would have forgotten anything so important.

When I relayed the session to David that evening, he suggested I stop seeing Dr. Singh. It drained me too much.

But part of me felt cleansed. I kidded him, "Where else do I get to talk only about me? I never ask how she is. It's completely selfish without guilt. Besides, I need help with my daughter and we still haven't talked enough about her."

"Why not?" David asked.

"I keep trying but she insists we dissect my family first." I paused, "She's twenty-six, you know."

David looked puzzled.

"My daughter."

He pulled me close.

"It's time. Next visit, I'll insist."

He kissed my cheek. "That's my girl. Now why don't we have some tea?"

"Is that the 'royal we' again," I laughed. "And which 'we' is going to make the tea this time?"

He smiled, "You, of course."

I punched his arm. "Honestly, it's going to take me fifty years to undo the damage your mother did."

As I headed towards the kitchen, it hit me. I turned back towards my smiling husband. This was no different than Dad clapping his hands at my mother. I suddenly realized she enjoyed getting his coffee just like I enjoyed making David's tea. It was

part of being a loving wife. I pretended to be annoyed with him. It was our playful game just as it had been with my parents. All those years, it was me who made it ugly. I was the one who turned their playful interaction into a fight.

CHAPTER 8

DAVID CALLED OUT from the side gate, "Honey, I'm home."

"Hi," I shouted back then returned to my gardening.

He pushed through the gate and noticed the old East Indian man digging beside me. "Who's that?" David nodded towards him.

"This is Koonar. He's helping me plant a garden." The old man looked up with a toothless smile. "Koonar knows so much about plants. They're male and female, you know. The holly bush is a 'he' and he wasn't happy until we cut back his dead branches."

"What's the mess in our driveway?" David asked.

"Topsoil."

"What's it doing there?"

"Where else could the truck dump it? Settle down, we'll bring it back here by wheelbarrow."

"What's this all about?" David asked.

"I was looking at some old photos of Dad and me working in the garden, covered in dirt. It was a paradise." David smiled his I-love-you-so-much-when-you're-happy smile.

"We're planting peonies. They remind me of Doug. I used to take them to the hospital when I visited him. Over there,

we're going to plant forsythia. It was the first thing to blossom in my father's garden every spring. I still get excited when it bursts out yellow each spring. Lilacs go in here."

David smiled again and said, "I've never heard you talk about your father like that."

"Dr. Singh helped me remember how much I loved working with Dad. I might even take some painting lessons."

I READ AN article called 'The Dead Mother Complex' which stated in most cases it is the mother who is at the root of the problem. But in my case, I realized it was my father. A French psychoanalyst, Andre Green, developed the theory. It was based on his research with people who had a deeply depressed parent. Green first discovered it in clients who came for treatment because they complained of a general impotence in their lives. His research was based primarily on people whose mother went into a depression typically because they miscarried or suffered from postpartum depression. Their children become deeply affected by this. The mother virtually stopped living and became seemingly dead to the world. A child whose mother had once been a source of vitality and happiness reacted when the mother withdrew. In my case, it was my father who became withdrawn. When I lost his affection, it deeply influenced my sense of self-worth. Perhaps that's why I wanted boy's attention as a teenager. The theory made sense to me.

CHAPTER 9

"SO HOW'D IT go today?" David asked when I returned from my session.

"She thinks I should try to find my daughter."

"Oh," David sat up. "And how do you feel about that?"

"Scared. What about you?"

He walked over and held me, "I want you to do whatever you need to do."

"When I started this whole Dr. Singh thing, I never expected to look for my daughter. I just wanted to address my feelings." I leaned into my husband. "I registered to find her years ago when she was twenty-one. If she had registered also, they would have connected us but she never did. I never told you."

"And now?"

"Dr. Singh wants me to go to Calgary. There's a place where birth parents and adopted children meet every year. Hundreds of them wander around the room checking each other out to see if someone resembles them in appearance. Weird, eh? But apparently lots of people attend every year."

"Are you going to do it?"

“No way!” I looked into his face. “Do you really think I could walk into a room full of strangers looking at me? I’d feel too exposed.”

“So what do you want to do?”

“I don’t know.” I searched his face for a negative reaction, “What if I really found her?”

David’s warm blue eyes indicated only support. “You’d like that, wouldn’t you? Let’s put your ghosts to rest.”

“What about the girls? They’d be horrified.”

“They’re teenagers, so no doubt it’ll come as a shock but they’ll get over it.”

“And your parents? How would they feel about me then?”

“You let me worry about my mom and dad.”

“Maybe I’ll run an ad in the personals. That’s about as public as I want to go. Her birthday is coming up. I could do it then.”

“Go for it. Let’s see if you find her first, then we’ll worry about telling people later.”

CHAPTER 10

Noel, born February 20, 1966.

I looked at the words on the page before me. Strange to see this string of letters formed in a way that revealed my deepest and most painful secret. My heart was pounding so hard, I was certain it would explode. Just sitting there was so confronting that I wasn't sure I could deal with the possibility of actually finding my daughter and going public with my past.

Noel born February, 20,1966

It was as though I was remembering another person, someone I knew long ago and had almost forgotten. Now with these words sitting so casually on the page, I was jolted back to the realities of my past.

Moments ago, my secretary had knocked and every molecule in my body pulsated in fear. Fear of what, I wondered. Being found out? Even if she had opened the door, she wouldn't know what I was writing. The look of guilt on my face would only indicate it was serious. Why on earth did I still feel guilt after all

these years? Especially when, David, whose opinion mattered most, was encouraging me. I had married the right person but what would everyone else think?

A tornado of emotions welled up uncontrollably as I thought of exposing my past to those I loved, my in-laws, Jeff, the girls. How would they take it? What about my friends and co-workers? My story would become a source of gossip. And would be pretty juicy stuff in our conservative, country club world.

I put the pen down. Alone in the confines of my office, the shame, the fear and years of longing wafted over me. Would my Noel want to meet me? Does she know she's adopted?

Yet, the words Noel, born February 20, 1966, challenged me. I picked up the pen. What the hell, I must get this out of my system once and for all. It probably wouldn't work but at least I will have tried.

Noel, born Feb. 20, 1966 Scarborough General Hospital. Please contact your birth Mother Box 1402, The Globe and Mail 444 Front St W Toronto ON M5V 2S9

I opened the newspaper and read my ad. I'd never find her with this. I should have spelled Noel as Noelle so the name looked like a girl's name. But that's not what I called her. The name in the ad looked like Noel as in Noel Coward. Maybe some young man would respond. Part of me felt relieved because I knew if she

answered, there would be no going back. Were David and I truly prepared for that?

Closing the paper, I turned back to my computer. The stock markets were up strongly.

CHAPTER 11

THEN THE WAIT began. I could no longer concentrate on my work, wondering if a letter had come. I wanted to sneak out midday and drive home to check the mail. It was torture.

It was snowing the day her letter finally arrived.

As I collected the mail, I didn't notice it. I sifted through the bills and junk advertising. Then I read the brown envelope with the Globe and Mail return address, it took a few seconds for me to realize what it was.

David had warned me not to get my hopes up. "There are lots of kooks in the world," he cautioned. "You must be careful, in case some kid writes just to cash in on a needy mother."

I walked across the entry, ripping the envelope open as I went. Inside was another envelope – a pink one. Still, I believed it was some boy named Noel answering. My heart held no promise.

I was standing on the bottom step when I began to read,

> ***In response to your Feb. 20 ad in the Globe,***
> ***I am an adopted person with the birth name***
> ***Noel, born Feb. 20,1966. To be sure that I am the***
> ***person you are looking for, could you please***
> ***write back with more details. My middle birth***
> ***name was MARKETTE.***

The railing held me up. I felt the way a tree must feel when hit by lightening, the charge jolting my entire being, yet I managed to remain standing. I'm sure my hair stood on end.

Oh, my God, it's her, my Noel. No one else knew her middle name, Markette, after her father. It was certainly not a name anyone could randomly guess. I held on to that railing for dear life.

Sometimes even now, I stand on that very step, remembering, unable to grasp the feeling entirely but enjoying the essence of shock, joy, fear, reality, God, my mother, fate – every emotion, every memory I felt in that moment of reading 'Noel Markette'. Dizzy, I sat on the step and continued her – my baby's letter.

> ***Please let me know if this is the person you are looking for and send the last name given to me at birth. My address to correspond is:***
>
> ***c/o Box 1933***
> **Canadian Champion News**
> **191 Main Street East**
> ***Milton, Ontario L9T 4N9***
>
> ***I hope to hear from you soon***
> ***If I am not the person you are looking for, I would appreciate it if you would take the time to respond anyway just to let me know.***

"Oh yes, you are the person I'm looking for," I spoke out loud as I held her letter close to my pounding heart. Unable to move from my spot, I envisioned her writing to me. TO ME! Her mother! Known to her after all. I held it as though it was my precious child herself twenty-seven years ago.

I imagined standing in the courtroom declaring "No, your Honor, I do not want to give away my baby." I was back at the foster mother's home holding my daughter. I could see her face peaking out of the pink snowsuit.

"I must find David." I ran into the den and picked up the phone, barely able to dial. Shaking, stuttering, I called his office. He was gone for the day.

I rang the country club and had him paged. The wait felt like an eternity.

"I'm sorry, he's not answering."

I tried several friends. They asked if I was okay. Yes, yes, I just need to find David. Do you have any idea where he might be?

I poured a drink, then another. I paced. I was getting drunk. I didn't care. This was worth celebrating. Where was my husband?

"Wake up." David shook me.

"Huh," I answered in a groggy voice.

"Why are you sleeping in your clothes? And so early?"

He looked concerned. My empty glass was on the night table. How many Black Russians had I drunk?

I bolted up, deranged and grabbed David's arm. "I found her," smiling so hard, I couldn't finish.

"Who?" he asked, perplexed.

"Noel, my daughter." Waiting for my husband to respond, I put both hands over my mouth, eyebrows raised.

He looked confused. I held my breath. He touched his chin thoughtfully, then the realization spread over his face. His expression changed to understanding, followed by a smile, then relief then fear – the same gambit of emotions I had felt earlier. Lowering his hands to his lap, he wet his lips, fidgeted with his shirt, first trying to tuck it in then pulling it out, taking off his tie. The suspense was killing me.

"Say something!" I understood where his thoughts were taking him, having spent the last few hours touring that terrain myself. The reality of a potential reunion with my daughter, unknown to us and our family, must be causing his emotions to swing. The consideration of how this news would affect everyone sobered any initial positive reaction.

Recovering, David hugged me. "That's great. I'm happy for you." Then almost hopefully, "Are you sure?"

I jumped out of bed and retrieved her letter. The stupor from drinking vanished as I showed it to him.

"Don't throw caution to the wind," his analytical lawyer's mind kicked in. "Make sure it's really her."

"Oh, I know it's her. She has too much information for it not to be. She knows her middle name. No one else knew that."

The next morning at work, I was exhausted from excitement, my late night talk with David and lack of sleep after tossing with dreams of my past, not to mention my hang over.

I settled into a boardroom chair, making sure the door was locked. I did not want to be disturbed. This would be the most important letter of my life. I must get it right, say what I needed to say without frightening her.

Staring at the empty page, I had no idea where to begin. I closed my eyes, rotated my neck, took a few deep breaths. "Mom, please help me. I'm so afraid." I prayed for the proper words. I sat for a few more moments, then began to write.

March 10,1993

Dear Noel

I can't believe that I am really writing this letter. It seems that you are my daughter. As long as there has been no mistake on your adoption papers, then I am certain you are who I'm looking for. I called you Noel Markette and surely there cannot be two of you born on Feb. 20/66. Markette is so unusual. I chose it because your father's name was Mark. My name at the time was Mott. Therefore, your birth name is Mott. I have been registered for several years with the adoption agency in Toronto for you to find me. I was advised that I could not receive information about you. I am a bit immobilized at receiving your letter. As soon as I read Markette, I knew it was you. I never really expected to hear from you. A part of me believed that you had died or some awful thing –

in a car accident. I never really believed I would find you. I also thought that if you were alive, most likely your parents might never have told you that you were adopted. I am so grateful to them for making this possible.

Noel, I don't know what to say to you about all this. What on earth do you say when you meet your daughter at 27? The only thing I know about you is that you have a brother – three years older, also adopted. I feel from your letter that you have come from a loving family. How on earth I can feel that from your letter, I don't know. I just pray that you have had a good life. I want to meet you, of course, as soon as possible – if you feel the same. I'm terrified and delighted about it. Please write me as soon as possible.

I live in Vancouver. I am a stockbroker. I have been married only once and for four years. I never was able to have other children. I do have two wonderful stepdaughters Shiera and Yael. They are 19 and 16. They are both ranked junior tennis players and have often played in the Canadian Nationals held in Milton. My husband, David, your stepfather, is a lawyer. He is taking this all very well and looks forward to our meeting. His family will be shocked of course. It all takes such getting used to. I have very little family myself. My brother, Jeff, your uncle, lives in Brampton. My older brother, Doug died but his wife and their son (21) live in Montreal. Both of my parents have passed away and only one aunt and uncle are alive.

I have enclosed a photo. It is the most recent taken on December 25,1992. It seems that I take all the pictures so I have few of myself. I almost chose an older photograph so I looked better. I also wanted a better one of David but I felt it more honest to send a recent one. What a shock for you to receive a photograph of me. I would like one of you also, of course.

Noel, years ago – 27 in fact – I was allowed to see you for three months before I signed the adoption papers. I went almost every day to the foster home. At the time, there was a song from West Side Story, which was popular. This song has always made me think of you. It went, "There's a time for us, a time and place for us. Someday, sometime, somewhere." The feelings I feel just knowing you are alive are so profound and the thought that I may soon meet you is overwhelming. I will be in Toronto in July but I would like to come sooner if it is agreeable to you. Please write back with your name and phone number so I can call you – and tell me something about yourself. I know you are wonderfully special. Thank you for answering the ad. It took nerve. Thank you. My life has changed dramatically. I must stop writing. Please write soon,

Love,

Margaret

(I find it difficult to say Mom as you must find it difficult to think of me in that way.)

CHAPTER 12

HE CRIED WHEN I told him. I've never seen him cry, not once in thirty-one years. Not when he was in the room with Mom when she died, not when we buried Doug or Dad but he cried the day I told him of the existence of his niece.

I met my brother, Jeff, in Las Vegas for an investment conference. With my daughter's letter in hand, the trip had taken on new meaning and I looked forward to spending time with him. It would be just the two of us, so I was certain things would go better than our last trip together. During that trip, we had taken our nephew James, Doug's son to New Orleans for his twenty-first birthday. I had been excited to spend quality time with James who looked so much like Doug at that age but Jeff brought his new wife, Monika along. Of course she should come, but no matter how hard I tried to like her, wanted to love my brother's choice, we just never connected. I couldn't imagine telling Jeff about my daughter with Monika there.

I arrived first and settled into the room we were sharing at the Monte Carlo Casino. We were there to inspect the mining properties of a public company, we had had our clients invest in. As I waited for Jeff to arrive, I worried over how my brother would handle this news. Perhaps he always knew and never mentioned it. He must have heard rumors.

My cheeks reddened. I needed to control the situation. My younger brother would surely be shocked to discover my past. Noel came with a steep price – exposure. I downed my drink and poured another.

***Should I tell him tonight*? I hadn't yet received her response to my letter. What if Noel never answered or worse, she met me and decided, 'well that was interesting' and, curiosity satisfied, walked out of my life? Perhaps I shouldn't tell anyone until I knew for sure we connected. But, I knew it wouldn't be fair to tell my brother such important news over the phone and this trip would be the only chance to do so in person.**

The door opened and there he was –with his blond hair, blue eyes and broad smile. He wore a pin stripped suit, having flown in straight from his Bay Street office. A five o'clock shadow darkened his face. Jeff reminded me a lot of Doug in appearance but he was already older than Doug when he died. It seemed impossible that almost twenty-two years had passed since my older brother died. Doug would have celebrated this day with me, I was sure. Perhaps he was. I smiled and looked skyward.

My hand trembled as I lifted my glass for one more swallow before I changed my brother's image of me forever.

I held my arms open. He dropped his bag and hugged me back. God, I've missed him. I lingered in his embrace, enjoying the feel of him. He pulled away embarrassed. Of course, he's a grown man and married. David had warned me to stop being a doting mother to my brother but I found it difficult to let go of this role.

"You've put on a little weight." I punched him in his tummy "Want a drink? I'm having a Black Russian."

"Sure. I'll have Scotch." I poured him a drink from the hotel bar fridge and sat on the bed twisting my wedding ring.

"You're fidgeting," Jeff observed.

"I have something to tell you. It's pretty big news. "Do you want me to tell you at the beginning or end of our trip?" It was selfish to hit him like this, but I couldn't help myself. "It's earth shatteringly big, actually," I paused so my words could sink in. Jeff stopped unpacking and turned with a surprised look. "Do you want me to tell you at the beginning or end of our trip?"

Curiosity sparked, he asked, "Are you pregnant?"

"No," I laughed, "but almost as good."

Jeff lowered himself on the other bed. "You better tell me. I can't wait until Sunday."

"Are you sure?"

"How do I know? Only you can answer that." He kicked off his shoes. "I'll let you know after you spill the beans."

My mouth opened but no words came out. Jeff waited until I gathered my nerve. "You know I grew up in the sixties."

Jeff nodded.

"I told you I never got into the drug scene. But, I was a product of the sixties in my own way, a flower child so to speak." I stopped and took a deep breath. "I had a baby. A daughter." I stopped to allow my words to register. I watched as his face stared blankly, then transformed into pure shock. "You never knew?"

"No." He exhaled and threw his head back. We sat in silence.

"I thought you might know. Someone could have told you. You were too young to remember, but I thought you might have heard the rumors."

"Never." He cleared his throat and sipped his scotch. His eyes held mine in disbelief. "Why are you telling me this now?"

"Because I found her. My daughter. Your niece."

"My niece," he repeated incredulous. "Where?"

"Milton."

"By the airport?"

"Yes."

"Jesus, I had no idea. When did this happen?"

"Finding her or having her?" I asked.

"Both."

"I've just heard from her. I ran an ad in the Globe and Mail. I have her letter with me. I'll read it to you if you like. I haven't met her yet and wouldn't have told you except we're here together and it seemed best to tell you in person."

"Hmm. I agree. I'm not sure how I would have handled a telephone call announcing a niece. When did you have her?"

"It was 1966. February 20th. I ran the ad on her birthday." It felt important to fill in the details. Although his face revealed little, I knew this had totally blown him away. I was prepared to answer his questions all night. It was only fair.

"So she's what? Twenty-seven?" It was more of a statement than a question, so I ignored it. "You weren't kidding when you said you had news."

"I wanted to tell you before but I was afraid. You looked up to me and frankly I didn't want to fall off the pedestal. Besides, it was this big family secret that no one ever mentioned, so it didn't feel fair to drag you into the past."

"Mom and Dad knew?" he asked, loosening his tie.

"Of course."

"Must have killed them."

"Yeah, it was pretty awful." I agreed.

He touched my hand, "And for you."

"Could have been worse," I smiled weakly. "In Nigeria, they stone unwed mothers to death." I cringed at calling myself an unwed mother in front of my brother.

"How old were you?"

"Sixteen. I didn't want to give her up for adoption but Mom and Dad made me. I had no choice. There were no abortions or birth control. It was a disgrace, the worse thing that could happen to a girl. Not like today. I could have run away, but what could I offer my daughter at that age?"

Jeff rose and sat beside me on my bed. He rested one hand on my shoulder. "I have a niece," he said simply. Tears formed uninvited. He wiped them unconsciously with the back of his hand. I leaned against my brother and we both wept.

"Maybe now you understand why I mothered you so much." I explained. "Poured all my maternal needs on you." He

wiped my tears gently with his fingers. "I don't even know if I'll get to meet her. I only have this letter, not even an address or her real name. I wrote to her through the Globe and can only wait and pray she contacts me again. You don't hate me do you?"

"For what?"

His question surprised me. "For never telling you? For being an unwed mother. For doing the most horrible thing a girl could do in the Sixties. For getting caught."

"Of course I don't hate you." His voice was soft and his blue eyes sparkled with moisture, "I just wish I had known. It's a real shocker." He straightened, "You could have told me, you know." His voice sounded hurt.

I touched his arm. "I never told anyone. I was so ashamed."

"Does David know?" he asked.

"Of course, I couldn't do this without his support. When I found out we couldn't have a baby, I was devastated. I went for counseling. The doctor convinced me I should try to find Noel. That's my name for her."

"Noel," he repeated, listening to the sound of the word.

"To give her up for adoption, I had to name her for the forms."

"Well this is news. I can't believe I never suspected."

"Me neither."

He lifted his glass in a toast, smiling and crying at the same time. "I'm very happy for you."

"Thank you."

"I'm not sure I should tell Monica. You know how she can be."

CHAPTER 13

THE FLIGHT HOME from Vegas had been delayed. Instead of arriving at two a.m., so I could get some sleep, the plane landed at six Monday morning, just in time for me to go to work. I went home at two that afternoon and was immediately asleep.

What the hell? It can't be morning already, I thought as I pulled the pillow over my head, but the sound continued. The clock said four o'clock. It took a moment to realize that it was the phone ringing and not my alarm, I rolled over and grab the phone, "Hello." It was only four o'clock the same afternoon.

"Hello, is this Margaret?" the voice asked.

"Yes"

"Hello," the voice repeated.

"Yes," I said louder this time. I felt groggy.

"My name is John. I've been asked to call you on behalf of a friend of mine. She lives in Milton, Ontario, and it seems you may be her birth mother."

"What?" I stuttered, my voice not in my control.

"Perhaps I have the wrong number," he said hesitantly.

"No, no. Give me a moment. I was asleep. Flew home late from Vegas. Worked all day. No sleep," Wake up, I commanded myself! You sound like an idiot. Pushing up on one arm, I shook my head. "Who is this?"

"John. A friend of Linda's. She asked me to call you."

"Sorry, I was out of it. It's okay now. I'm awake, sort of."

"I can call back if you prefer." the voice said.

I sat up. "No, please give me a minute."

"Linda asked me to meet with you," John continued.

"Linda?"

"Yes, you ran an ad..."

"Her name is Linda?"

"Oh I'm sorry, perhaps I'm out of line here. I should call back later."

"No, please don't hang up. You want to meet me?"

"Yes, Linda asked me to. On her behalf."

"Where are you?"

"I work at Richmond Chrysler. I could come over after work. Around six?"

"Oh God, I'm a mess." Wide awake now, I swung my legs over the side of the bed and took a deep breath. "Could we meet tomorrow, instead?" I walked towards the door then back into the room and sat on the bed. "I need some time." ***Stop it, you sound ridiculous.*** **"I must sound like some old drunk or something."**

"No, not at all, not now that you have explained. Tomorrow's fine. I'll come by after six."

"Do you know where I live?"

"Yes, the address was on your letter."

"Right. Okay, I'll see you tomorrow."

"Bye."

I was wide awake. His phone call destroyed any chance of sleep as the adrenaline took over and our conversation sunk in. John, a friend of my daughter's. Linda. Noel is Linda. I couldn't wait. I looked up Richmond Chrysler in the phone book, grateful I remembered in my groggy state and called John back and arranged for him to come after work that day. Next, I called

David and asked him to come straight home.

JOHN ARRIVED AT six-thirty. I had changed three times, wanting to look my best for this bearer of news about my daughter. He would be my judge. I splashed my face with cold water and spent more time than usual on my make-up, trying to look presentable on no sleep and frazzled nerves. David tried to calm me but I was a lost cause.

"How can I possibly be calm?" I said. David smiled, enjoying

my happiness. The doorbell rang. "You answer it."

John entered. Tall, thin, a kind face. He smiled. I walked towards him and held out my hand, "Hi, I'm Margaret," I tried to make my voice gracious. "Come in."

We sat in the living room where he watched me intently. Stared actually. "May I get you a drink? Coffee? A beer?" I asked.

"I'd love a beer." He responded.

I turned toward the bar then stopped and looked back at John. With a deep breath, I confessed, "I'm so nervous. My life is in your hands. Please like me. I have to pass this test!"

He smiled. "You're doing fine. I'm just a little stunned myself. You look so much like her."

"I do?" A smile escaped my lips. I relaxed a little.

John pointed to a photograph of me on the piano. "That could be Linda. It's mind boggling actually."

"Really?" I looked at the photo of me at age thirty-nine. I had wanted to test the photographers before I chose them for our wedding. This was David's favourite and he insisted it be placed prominently on my mother's piano. "Let me get those drinks. I think we could all use one. Then I want to hear everything."

Over beer, John told us about my Noel. "She's married to a great guy, Peter. We worked together in Toronto."

"What does Peter do?"

"He's a mechanic at Air Canada now but we worked together at Golden Mile Motors."

"Golden Mile, that's close to where I grew up."

"Really? She grew up in Scarborough. They're in Milton now."

The thought that she had been so close to me filled me with wonder as well as sadness.

"She graduated from the University of Toronto. Scarborough campus, I think."

“Scarborough campus! That’s within walking distance to my parents house. I could have bumped into her. I could have walked right past her without knowing."

"This must be tough for you." he said. It said something about her to have a sensitive friend like this. “You won't be disappointed. Everyone loves Linda. She’s special. Beautiful, kind, generous. I can't wait to tell her about you. She wants me to call her as soon as I leave."

"She's waiting for your call?" I sat up surprised and looked towards David.

"Yes, she went for a horseback riding lesson and asked me to call her after."

"I love horse back riding." I said, smiling at David who sat by the piano like a Cheshire Cat, taking in everything.

"Peter works nights, so his mother is taking care of the baby while she’s riding.”

"The baby! She has a baby?” I turned towards David. “Oh my God, I'm a grandmother!"

“I’m married to an old woman,” David teased.

I waved at him to stop.

"I shouldn’t have told you. I don't want to ruin it for Linda. I'm sure she wants to tell you everything herself."

"A grandmother, isn't it wonderful?"

David nodded in agreement.

"Peter, Linda's husband,” John continued, “wanted me to meet you as a preliminary precaution. He was concerned about who you were. With a little one, he felt that he should check you out before allowing you into their lives. He's very protective."

"So was David. He worried some welfare kid would show up and take advantage of us."

"You don't have to worry about that. They’re doing well. They own their own home and work hard. You're going to like them a lot."

"You better tell them the truth about Margie, though," David interrupted.

We turned towards David. "What?" I asked.

"She's a raging alcoholic," he said.

"Oh please!" I threw the cushion at him. "Don't listen to

him." I told John in a worried tone, while I shot David a dirty look.

"David, this is serious especially when you consider how I must have sounded on the phone when John called." I turned back towards John. "I want to meet her as soon as possible."

"I'm sure they want to meet you, too. Peter works for the airlines so they can fly out pretty easily. In fact, they come to Vancouver a lot. They love it here."

He stood, "I should go and report in. It's ten o'clock in Toronto so Linda's probably home by now and sitting beside the phone waiting. I don't want to spoil it for her by telling you too much. You two will have a lot to talk about."

"Call me and let me know, will you? I'm very anxious."

"Sure, but I think Linda will want to call you herself."

CHAPTER 14

THE WAIT WAS hell. David sat quietly in front of the television watching wrestling. "How can you just sit there?" I asked, exasperated. "And wrestling of all things.

I paced up and down the den, jumping every time the phone rang. David's friend called to arrange a golf game and I thought I would die until he hung up. I signaled for him to get off the phone. Then the phone would sit silently, tormenting me.

"What did John tell her?" I wondered out loud. "Did he say I was nice? Perhaps he told her not to call."

David assured me that I behaved just fine. "She'll be thrilled to find someone like you."

"I didn't really believe it was happening and now everything is going so fast," I confessed. "Maybe I should tape our phone call?" But I didn't know how to work the answering machine. I searched for the owner's manual while David sat grinning as though he enjoyed my anxiety.

I found myself critiquing everything about myself. The next day, I'd start running. I'd lose weight, get my hair cut. I felt like a teenager again preparing for her first prom date.

"How can you just sit there!" I shouted at David again. He stood and took me in his arms, laughing, and kissed the top of my head.

"Will she let me fly to Toronto right away? I told John I was going in July but I can't wait that long."

When the phone rang, an earth quake of emotions opened under me. "You answer it."

"It's her," he said, holding the phone out to me.

"I'll take it in the bedroom." I turned to run up the stairs, two at a time.

Unable to move, I sat on the edge of the bed and stared at the phone. My body felt paralyzed but inside everything was in flux.

"Margie, are you going to pick up the phone?" I heard David calling from the bottom of the stairs.

Cautiously, as if my life depended on it, I picked up the receiver. "Hello." It was just a whisper.

"Hello," her voice beckoned from three thousand miles away. Silence. My vocal chords wouldn't work.

"Hello," she repeated.

Come on, say something, an inner voice commanded me. Still no words came out.

"Hello," she said again, "This is Linda. My friend John was just there. Don't you know who this is?"

"Oh, I know exactly who this is. I just don't know what to say." I whispered. It felt as though my words were coming from someone else. Someone I knew long ago. A sad, young girl, alone at the foster mother's home, singing to her baby so that no one would hear. It was as though I was in that room again, holding her.

"I know. This is strange, isn't it?" Noel said. "I'm really nervous too. It's all happening so fast. I just got your letter today. I was going to wait a few days and think about everything, but Peter called John and arranged for him to visit while I was out riding. When John called and told me that you were expecting my call, I freaked." She stopped for a moment, "I don't know what to say to you either."

After a brief silence, the words started to flow between us.

"I can't believe I'm talking to you. I was terrified John wouldn't like me." I confessed.

"You gave him a beer, so don't worry, you passed with flying colors."

"Thank God I had beer in the house." I said. "You have no idea what this means to me."

"Me, too. I've always wondered about you," Noel said.

"You knew about me? Your parents told you that you were adopted?"

"Yes. They told me from the beginning. I knew even before I understood what adopted meant."

"That's wonderful. I thought you didn't know."

Linda, began talking and couldn't stop. Neither could I. She told me how she knew her name was Noel and as a child, she got mixed up and told her friends that Linda meant Christmas in French.

"What nationality am I? Am I French? I've always wondered," she asked.

"Yes, a long way back, on my Dad's side." I talked about

Mom and Dad and Doug. "You have an uncle in Toronto, Jeff. He got married recently. I know you have a brother. The foster mother told me about him."

"At first I thought you meant you had given up a son for adoption. I got mixed up and was excited to hear I had another brother but my husband figured out that you meant Paul, the son my parents adopted before me."

"You have no other siblings. I couldn't have more children although I wanted to. But you have two step sisters, Shiera and Yael."

"Sisters!" she almost screamed. "I've always wanted a sister and now I have two. I can't wait to meet them."

I went on to tell her about my infertility and how I went to Dr. Singh.

We discovered that I begun therapy at the same time that she registered to find me.

Noel told me, "I went to Children's Aid when I was sixteen, but when I got home and told my parents that I was registering to find my birth mother, they had a fit. So I never followed through. I wouldn't have registered if they hadn't given

me their approval when I had Cassandra. That's your granddaughter's name."

"My granddaughter." I repeated her name, "Cassandra."

"The day after Cassandra was born, my parents came to the hospital with my adoption papers. They had read that when an adopted woman has a baby, it becomes important for her to find out about her family history. It's true. The doctors kept asking me if I had a family history of this or that and it made me cry not knowing."

"I can imagine. It must have been awful."

"It was. I worried about my baby. I wanted to know she would be healthy and there wasn't anything in her family history I should know about."

"There isn't. We're all healthy. I always tell David my ancestors built this country whereas, most of David's family was killed in Russia during the pogroms, so he doesn't know about them either. He doesn't even know his real name."

"Really?"

"It's true. His grandfather was given a new Anglo-Saxon name when he came to Canada in 1916 because the immigration

official couldn't pronounce his Russian one. The real family name was lost when his grandfather died. David asked of course but his grandfather insisted his only name was his Canadian one. So he sort of understands what it must have been like for you."

I caught sight of David peeking around the door. "Please don't listen." I waved him away. "It makes me nervous!"

"Is he listening to us?" Noel asked.

"Yes, he's so excited. I don't know what I would do if he didn't support me in finding you. I'm a lucky gal."

"I waited for Peter to leave for work. He works the night shift at Air Canada. He would have stood over me when I called and I couldn't stand that."

"Do you get airline passes?"

"Yes."

"Fabulous. When can you visit? I have to meet you."

"Actually, we've discussed it. We might be able to come next weekend," she said.

"Oh, my God." I felt panic and delight all at once. "Next weekend! "

"John told me that you called him back and wanted to

meet right away. That's just like me. I couldn't wait either. Peter is so cautious. He wanted me to go slow but now that I know where you are, I can't wait."

She said she was just like me! Her words became music, a symphony, composed exclusively for me, each note vibrated my own Ode To Joy.

Two hours flew by. I told Noel I would call her back so the cost was on my phone bill. "Don't worry about it," she said. "This is just as important to me. I have thought about you so much over the years. I felt you missing me. It started every Christmas, probably because you called me Noel, but I could feel you needed me."

"It's true."

"The feeling would last until my birthday each February. I thought about you other times, of course, but it was especially strong then. I was surprised in your letter when you said that you had visited me for the first three months."

"They told me not to but I went anyway."

"Maybe that's why I felt your pain all these years. They say a baby really bonds with its mother the first three months."

She paused. “My parents told me that they didn't pick me up until I was three months old. They said it was because you could change your mind. They could have had me right away, but were told you could take me back and they said they wanted to wait until they knew they could keep me. It would be too hard on them otherwise."

"Yes, it would have been hard. I know. You were a beautiful baby and you're very beautiful now according to John."

"Oh brother, what did he tell you? I may not live up to his description," she said in a worried tone.

"You won't disappoint me. I want to know everything about you. Absolutely everything. Do your parents know that we’ve made contact?"

"Yes, it was my dad who found the ad. I wouldn't have thought about looking in the newspaper. Did you run it every year?"

"No, this was the first time"

"No kidding? The first time. That's amazing, but then Dad told me that he checked every year. When he saw it, he showed my mother and they discussed it for a few days before

they told me."

"I am so grateful to them. They must be amazing people to have given the ad to you. I'm sure it upset them."

"Yeah, they are nice. They were upset at first and weren't sure whether to tell me but then they decided that this was something I needed. They knew it was a real possibility with all the reunions that are going on now."

"You tell them for me that I am very, very grateful. This is the biggest gift that anyone has ever given me."

"They know that, but then you gave them a pretty big gift also. My parents always said you must be the most generous person in the whole world to give your baby away to a family who needed one so badly." I felt my eyes water. She paused, caution in her voice. "Can I ask you about my father?"

"Yes. Of course, you want to know about him. I wish I could tell you we were childhood sweethearts but we weren't." I went on to tell her what I could about her father. Later, when I received the first photographs from Linda, I would discover how much Mark looked like her husband, Peter. "I have no idea what happened to him. A marriage between us would never have

worked. I'm sorry."

"I got my parents. Thank you. Thank you for my parents. I have always wanted to thank you for giving me my parents. Thank you. There, I said it, finally."

"You are too good to be true." Years of guilt vanished with her words, so simple yet so freeing, like a convict escaping from prison after years of torture. "Weren't you ever angry at me?"

"No," her response was definite. "My parents told me from the beginning what it was like for an unwed mother in those days. My parents always said you gave me up so I could have a better life. I really appreciate and value that."

I tried to picture her. Where was she sitting? What did she look like? "How tall are you?"

"Five, four and three quarters."

"Oh, you're shorter than me. John told me that we looked a lot alike."

"He told me that there was no mistaking you were my mother."

"David said your handwriting looked just like mine."

"I'm left-handed so my writing is slanted."

"So am I! The only one in my family." This information felt important somehow, like espionage secrets acquired by foreign agents. The more I heard similarities, the happier I became, beaming like a mother watching her newborn smile.

"What else did John tell you?"

"He was very hesitant to say too much. He said you were working on your accounting designation. I took two years of the CGA course, but I got too busy as a stockbroker to finish. He said that you majored in languages. And Cassandra," I inhaled excitedly, " I'm a grandmother. Wow, I've always wondered about that. Incredible. A daughter and granddaughter in one fell swoop."

"Did he tell you everything about me?" her voice sounded a little disappointed.

"No, he refused because he didn't want to rob us of the pleasure of discovering each other."

"That's good. I don't want to be a disappointment in any way. I can't trust him not to build me up too much."

"Nothing you do could disappoint me. It's a dream just to

hear your voice. I never thought it would happen. Be prepared for the biggest hug of your life!"

"I'm looking forward to long talks together," Linda said.

"Me too."

Neither of us wanted to hang up. I was afraid if I did it might just be a dream. I couldn't bear to lose her again. Not now, not after hearing her voice. Imagine! I knew it was selfish to keep holding on. We were both getting delirious and kept repeating ourselves. It is so nice to talk to you. Did I tell you...this and that. Eventually not making much sense with our words, but sort of purring.

David continued to eavesdrop. I tried to ignore his presence and concentrate on my daughter's every word. Rejoicing at her deep throaty laugh so similar to my kid brother, loving her pleasure in talking to me, cherishing the snippets of information about herself. She was real. My Noel was real and alive and happy to talk to me.

She had grown up so close to my parent's home and she knew my last name. Her parents told her the name I gave her on the adoption papers including my maiden name. She even looked

it up in the phone book when she was a teenager. What would I have done if she had called back then? What would my parents have done? There were so many questions but I had to let her sleep. It was two a.m. in Toronto.

Finally, I let her go and said good night.

CHAPTER 15

I WATCHED AS my stepdaughter, Yael, talked on the phone to one of my clients. She was giving quotes on the stock market. I was proud of her, the interest she showed in becoming a broker after she graduated. It would be three years before she started university, but it made me happy that she wanted to follow in my footsteps, taking over my practice in the future. Shiera often said Yael was more like me than the rest of the family, that somehow her personality had been altered by knowing me. Yael seemed to assume ownership of me the same way that Shiera assumed ownership of David. She would confide in me like an ally, not like a step-parent. We were close and it was going to surprise her to discover that she didn't really know me at all.

Looking at her now with her cute, freckled face, turned up nose and blue eyes, I knew I couldn't leave it any longer. It was the next step. She would be shocked for sure, but would her feelings for me change? I hoped not.

Just thinking about exposing myself, I felt shaky and nauseous. David wanted to tell her himself but I insisted that it

had to be me. I couldn't resist patting her on the head. She looked up, surprised at my sudden show of affection. I will tell her tonight, I decided.

David had called his parents last night and broke the news to them. Amazingly, they were terrific. There was no way they could have been prepared for anything like this and I'm sure it shocked them but they telephoned right away to congratulate me. I imagined my mother-in-law standing over her husband telling him to be nice. And he was.

Shiera had suspected my story. We were having a quiet dinner together three years earlier when she was fifteen and gushing over some boy at school so I gave her a coming-of-age lecture. She had rolled her eyes, "Yeah, yeah, don't worry." Then the words just came out, "Trust me, I know."

A smart girl, she stopped and stared, "And?"

"Nothing," I replied, "just be careful," but she guessed by my tone that there was much more.

THE TIME HAD arrived. Yael was settled on the couch watching, Days of Our Lives, when I walked into the den. Little

did she know that she was about to experience her own personal soap opera. Her face was so innocent, so protected from the real world. At fifteen, all kids want their parents to be normal. Yael got embarrassed if she thought David and I were the least bit conspicuous. She would roll her eyes and say 'Please' in that long drawn out way that let us know she didn't approve.

"Yael would you mind turning the T.V. off? I need to speak with you." She started to protest, but the tone of my voice must have conveyed importance.

"What is it?" she asked cautiously. "Did someone die? Your voice is scaring me."

"God no. It's nothing to be frightened of but I just hope you find it in your heart to understand." Yael sat up hugging a throw pillow.

I repeated the same story I told my brother about not doing drugs. "But I did experience the sixties in my own way. I guess I was a bit of a flower child. You see, I had a baby." I waited for the words to sink in. Yael looked perplexed at first then the shock spread visibly over her face. "I gave her up for adoption and I've just found her."

Her eyes opened wide in horror.

I lowered my head and fidgeted with my hands, repeating. "I had a baby and I've found her." With a deep breath, I faced my stepdaughter. "We're meeting next week. She'll be here. She lives in Toronto with her husband."

"What are you telling me?" she said. "Does Dad know?"

"Of course. I would never try to find her without his agreement."

"I can't believe you never told me," she said in her long drawn out this-is-inappropriate-behavior voice, letting go of my hands.

I sat quietly, taking in her features, blues eyes straining, hands on her waist, leaning away from me as though I was a stranger. I moved away, straightening. "I never told anyone. Not even my brother. I only told him when we were in Las Vegas. He was extremely surprised and upset that I hadn't told him. I couldn't. I was very ashamed. It was a secret."

"When did you tell Dad?"

"He's always known. I couldn't have not told him. It's part of who I am. I told him long before we were married." Yael

stood and started pacing, my words creating a new reality for her world.

“Have you or Dad told Shiera?”

“She guessed.”

“What!” Yael stopped and faced me. “Shiera knew and I didn’t?” I explained the conversation I had with her sister a few years ago and how she came to suspect.

“I can’t believe no one told me.” Yael sat on the couch. "I want to know right now if there are any other skeletons in our closet.” She was deservedly angry. “I do not want any other surprises in my life. Tell me now if there is anything else I should know."

"No, there's nothing else. This is plenty."

Yael faced me, her eyes fixed on mine. I was prepared to let her vent. I waited for her rage. "I never thought we had skeletons in our closet. I didn't even think we had a closet!"

Geez, what a gal, I thought. She kept her sense of humor in the midst of all this. "I love you." I hugged her, laughing. “You know, Yael, if someone has no skeletons, then their lives are probably boring. It means they haven’t lived.”

"Oh, so you're telling me to go and get some skeletons!"

"No, of course not, just to live your life fully."

"Boy, have you caught me off guard. Are you sure there's nothing else? I'd rather get it all over with at once."

I shook my head. "I assure you that I am the only one in this family with skeletons. Do you hate me?" She shook her head. There was no condemnation. Only support from her, from David's parents, my brother. "I wouldn't hurt you for the world. I should have told you, but I didn't think I would ever see my daughter again. And now she's coming here. With her husband and my granddaughter." Yael looked up. "Yes, you heard right, my granddaughter. She has a daughter. I am so happy. Please tell me you're okay."

"Baba, you're a Baba. Oh, my God. Tell me everything," she said pulling me back down on the couch and snuggling in. God, I love her, I thought, as the words of a lifetime poured out. I should have done this years ago.

CHAPTER 16

THE NEXT DAY, I received phone calls from various members of my new son-in-law Peter's family. Cecile, his mother, told me she had lost a child who died of illness at the age of three. This bonded us instantly.

Peter's Aunt Charlotte couldn't wait for me to meet Linda to see how beautiful she was, so she called to say she was faxing a photograph to my office.

That day the Dow was crashing and other brokers were in a panic, but I didn't care. I stood rooted in front of the fax machine waiting for a picture of my daughter. Nothing else mattered. This was much more exciting than the price of IBM.

A co-worker came up to use the fax machine.

"I could be awhile. I'll do it for you." I took his papers. I didn't want anyone standing over me. I glanced around to make sure no one was watching. My heart was palpitating. Shaky, I observed my shy self. Interesting. Why should I care what people think? The sound of the fax starting its transmission drew my attention back.

Breathless, I watched as her image flowed out of the machine. I was surprised to see a mature woman staring back at me. She looked so, so... so grown up! What did I expect? A baby? She was lovely but the face looking up at me was not of a twenty-seven year old. She looked at least thirty-five. Not a little girl at all. I can't be this person's mother? The fax was dark and unclear. I studied it closely. This woman was an executive. Confident. Someone who ran a big corporation or something. Suddenly, I felt quite inadequate.

"Who's that?" one of the accounting clerks asked, peering over my shoulder.

I grabbed the picture close to my body. "No one." She shrugged. I felt the red flush spreading over my cheeks. "Sorry. Go ahead, I'm finished." She placed her fax on the machine.

I sat at my desk and stared at my lost daughter's image. The noise in the office escalated as the Dow broke one hundred points on the downside. Brokers passing my desk probably wondered how I could sit there with this ridiculous look on my face when their world was crashing. Well, mine was out of control.

Charlotte telephoned. "Isn't she beautiful?"

"Yes," I whispered, still in shock.

"We all love Linda," she continued. "You're very lucky to find a daughter like her."

"Yes, I know," I said, staring at the image of my Noel. Who is this person? Will she like me or be disappointed?

I picked up the phone. "Charlotte faxed me your picture. You're so grown up."

"What did you expect," Linda asked, "a baby?" My words exactly.

We confirmed her arrival time and I hung up, not wanting to be a pest. I had called her so often this week.

I sat staring at the fax. Did I really expect a carbon copy of myself? She didn't look as much like me as I had expected or as her friend, John, had implied. I'm not sure I would have recognized her if we had passed on the street.

"JEFF PHONED ME today." Linda's voice spoke to me from across the miles. "He's anxious to meet me. I'm dying to meet my

uncle but it doesn't feel right before I meet you. I told him to wait 'til we get back from Vancouver."

I wish she hadn't.

"HI, IT'S PETER."

"Peter," I replied happily. "Hello. This is wonderful. A phone call from my new son-in-law. To what do I owe this pleasure?"

"Don't get too excited. I'm calling with some bad news."

My heart clunked like a faulty transmission in an old car. "What is it?" I stood, gripping the kitchen counter.

"I'm calling because we may not be able to come after all." My knees buckled. "Linda didn't want to upset you until we knew for sure but I felt I should warn you. Her parents called today and they were upset about us visiting you. Linda drove over to see them. I'm sure we'll work it out, but she doesn't feel she can go right now without their approval."

Not wanting Peter to sense my fear, I asked, "Is she all right?" I couldn't stand it if I didn't meet her. My vulnerability

bubbled up like a geyser. I'd told so many people. I shouldn't have said anything. I felt so exposed.

"She's been crying all day. She really wants to come. She's dying to meet you and personally I think she will come anyway even if they don't want her to. It's too late to turn back now that she has spoken to you. She needs to meet you as much as you do her, but she feels guilty."

"I don't want her to upset them. I wouldn't hurt her parents for the world."

"Neither would she. Don't worry. I just wanted to prepare you in case we had to cancel. We'll come another time, if not now."

"Thanks, Peter, for letting me know. Keep me informed, will you?"

"Sure."

I managed to keep my voice steady but the minute we hung up I fell apart. She was so close, within my grasp. My world shifted again. No longer solid, the earth quaked and became loose. I sat down unable to concentrate, tears falling involuntarily. I couldn't make them visit and wished I hadn't told anyone until

we had met. I'd disrupted everyone's life. What a fool I was.

CHAPTER 17

MY BABY IS arriving today. Her parents came round. Thank God it was only a moment of panic. Who could blame them?

We should have bought shares in Bell Telephone, we had called so often. I phoned every day, partly to make sure she hadn't changed her mind, but mainly because I did not want a day to pass, ever again, that I did not know where my daughter was or what she was doing. She was very patient with me.

And now she would be here any minute. Other than her parent's initial moment of panic, everything had gone smoothly and quickly, our meeting seemed pre-ordained.

My grief washed away like a mountain river, flowing quietly and freely over the rocks, all obstacles overcome as though they were not there. That's how my pain dissolved, easily, naturally. A new life, rewritten, the old plot put back on the shelf rejected. I decided I liked this story after all.

I had had my hair permed the day before and hated the results. It was too frizzy and not me at all. Why did I take a chance on my appearance at a time like this? No matter what I

tried, I couldn't calm my hair or my nerves. I wished I was prettier, smarter, nicer, richer; better in every way. I wanted to be perfect. For her to be proud of me.

I changed my clothes five times, settling for a plain black pant suit. There was no time left to alter my appearance. This is it, this is me, frizzy hair and all.

David drove to the airport to pick up them up. I couldn't go with him. I couldn't meet her in a crowded airport. This was too private an affair to display before the world. I WAS MEETING MY NOEL TODAY. MARCH 30,1993. A day I would cherish forever.

The table was set for lunch with my best dishes, hand painted in Israel with purple placemats to match, my first extravagant purchase as a broker, fourteen years ago, saved for special occasions. What could be more special than this?

Earlier as I prepared the lunch, a gambit of emotions overtook me. I had carried my secret, trying to maintain power over my universe, and now suddenly, I was no longer master. Once I had revealed the truth, I metamorphosed back into an adolescent with no ability to anticipate what popped out of my

mouth.

While setting the table, giggles bubbled up involuntarily from deep inside. Emotions exploded like fireworks on the First of July. It was the First of July. It was Christmas, Thanksgiving and my birthday - a celebration of life, my life, my baby's life. It was miraculous awe, laughter and fear.

I observed these conflicting feelings with curiosity. There were still some negative emotions despite my joy. I had learned to hide my feelings for so long that I sometimes forgot how to enjoy life, feel it, welcome it. This moment then that moment, again and again. Come on, I thought, open up, enjoy, allow yourself to be fully happy.

The eggplant I had cut with love and placed in a marinade, sat forgotten as I became lost in the realization that I was cooking lunch for my daughter! I shook my head and observed the dining table with a smile.

Lunch could not describe the banquet I was preparing. This celebration was nothing less than a blessing through food. An offering of who I was. Smoked salmon with miniature bagels and cream cheese, fresh shrimp drenched in my father's seafood

sauce recipe, an assortment of sushi, smoked meats, croissants, three varieties of breads, potato salad, watercress salad, cheese platter, grilled vegetables, fruits, red and white wine. All ready for my daughter. Beer and champagne were cooling on ice. It was my attempt to be perfect. Everything lay ready. I didn't want to interrupt the action to serve lunch. Not today.

I just hoped I wouldn't slobber all over her like a love sick fool. Calm. I must stay calm - my mantra for today.

UP THE STAIRS. Down the stairs. Where should I be when she arrived? Should I make my entrance coming down the staircase like Scarlett O'Hara in Gone With The Wind? Or should I be sitting calmly on the couch and rise graciously when they came through the door? I was too nervous to make a gracious entrance. Pacing, I went over my possibilities, rehearsing my lines.

The car. They're here. I ran to the window. Oh my God, oh my God. I rushed to the door and pulled it open. It banged against the wall. I was in the driveway. I had given myself brilliant dialogue, but my entire script was forgotten as soon as I

laid eyes on her perfect face. Beautiful, she's beautiful! Her face turned towards mine as she emerged from David's Jeep. She didn't look at all like the mature woman in the faxed photo. Her appearance was much younger. Yes, this is my daughter.

Slowly, hesitantly, a smile spread from her lips to her eyes. Standing beside the car, we stared at each other nervously, appraising the reflection of ourselves.

She was shorter than me. Her blonde hair was long and straight, the way mine used to be at her age. Slim, young, her face was soft with dimples and high cheek bones. Her skin was slightly tanned.

No longer able to restrain myself, I grabbed onto her allowing all the sorrows of my past to release. Laughing. Crying. I hugged her, then held her at arms length, "Look at you. You're beautiful. Oh, David, isn't she beautiful." I laughed.

"Hi," She hugged me shyly.

Peter got out of the car. I observed he was tall and skinny with thick, dark hair. A video camera hid his face. "She wouldn't even wait for me to get out of the car. How am I supposed to film

this?"

The camera was pointing at us. I became embarrassed. I knew I was out of control, behaving like a character in Yael's Game Boy, bouncing up and down so caught up in a game where I didn't yet know the rules. Throwing my arms around him, I kissed my new son-in-law. Who should I hold first? I tried to envelope them both.

I pushed the video camera aside, so I could see his face. Slim, dark features, bushy eyebrows; a strong face, a kind face full of amusement at my reaction. I looked back and forth between them. My Noel smiled her smile as big as the sun. It was like seeing myself twenty years ago. Thank God, she looks like me.

"Look at you," I repeated in awe.

"Hi," she responded.

Then there was silence. A turmoil of emotion hung in the air as I looked into her eyes and saw the lost innocence of my youth like a mirror. The beauty of innocence. Holding her tight, I never wanted to let go.

"Cassandra," Linda said. "You must meet your

granddaughter." She pulled away and went to the car. Cassandra, sat in a car seat they had brought with them on the plane. She was eight months old, dressed in a bright flowered coat. My new granddaughter had a upturned nose and blonde hair. She was the image of my Noel, of me as a baby and of my mother and grandmother. All of the old black and white photographs I had treasured for years were encompassed in their faces.

"Hello," I half expected her to answer back as I took her out of her car seat and turned towards David. "Say hello to your new step granddad." Laughter, Linda's and mine.

David tickled Cassandra under her chin, "Chubby."

"Chubby! She's not chubby." I pulled Cassandra close to my body with a mock look of disgust. "Be quiet. She's beautiful. She's perfect. Maybe your babies were chubby but mine are perfect!" I clung to my new granddaughter.

Linda said, "I think these cheeks must run in the family. I have them too." I stopped and looked at my daughter. I touched her face. "She's gorgeous," I repeated turning to David. "Just gorgeous."

At first, I found it difficult to look at Cassandra because she reminded me so much of what I had lost in giving up my daughter, Noel. I needed to push those thoughts away since they wouldn't do me any good. I reminded myself to enjoy her as Linda now. Dwelling on the past accomplishes nothing.

The hum of Peter's camera was the only sound. There was a pregnant silence. Pregnant. Oh my God. Noel was pregnant. She saw me staring at her tummy. She was several months pregnant.

"Yes. That was my surprise. I'm due in September. I didn't want John to tell you!"

"Pregnant!" I turned to David, "She's pregnant. Oh my God, We're going to have another grandchild!"

David smiled at me lovingly. "We should call the paper. Stop the presses, stop the presses! Have I got a story! Save the back page!" I punched him in the arm as he burst into his typical laughter.

The two guys stood enjoying our pleasure, our discovery, as though they had set everything up themselves. I touched her tummy. "A baby. I'm going to have a baby."

"No. I'm going to have the baby," Noel corrected me.

"Of course. You're going to have the baby. I mean, we're going to have a new grandchild. It's going to be a boy."

"I hope so, but we don't know. I told the nurse at the ultra sound not to tell me."

"It's going to be a boy. I know."

"How?"

"I just know. That's all. I'll tell you why later. We have plenty of time to talk. A lifetime! Now let's go inside and have lunch. I hope you're hungry."

"Margie has been fussing over this lunch all week. There's enough food for ten people." David held the front door open.

I kept staring at my daughter over lunch. Embarrassed, she would look away. I tried to stop but couldn't. It was eerie to see her looking so much like me at that age.

"You're staring again," she turned shyly but the pleasure on her face was similar to that of a teenage girl who caught a boy eyeing her at a school dance.

"How can I stop? You're really, really here. It's

amazing." She smiled back knowingly and looked at her own baby.

Linda was around the same height as my mother. Her blonde hair was cut into short bangs at the front. She had my nose, turned up, a miniature ski jump. Cassandra had the same nose.

Linda informed me that her braces were new. I thought they make her look twelve which was a relief after feeling intimidated by the faxed photo. She was prettier than the picture, soft and kind. A light blue flowered maternity smock covered her pregnant tummy which was just beginning to show. Cassandra pulled at her mother's hair while she sat on her mother's lap. Her laugh was identical to my brother, Jeff's laugh.

Picking at my food, absorbed in the moment and the wonder, I was unable to eat.

Linda served herself marinated eggplant, "My favorite," she announced. I beamed.

David told funny stories to break the ice and the uncomfortable silences during which I continued to gaze longingly at Linda, wanting to hug her again. His words

weren't particularly funny but when David laughed, you had to respond, his was so infectious.

"Did you hear the one about the grasshopper that went into a bar? The bartender said, 'Hey we have a drink named after you.' The grasshopper said, 'oh you have a drink named Kevin?'"

"Oh, David. He tells these terrible jokes all the time. Actually the bar jokes are from Yael. When David calls his girls, he doesn't even say hello. He starts every call with, did you hear the one about the... whatever the joke du jour is."

"We laugh the same," my daughter noted. "We start and stop at exactly the same time. It's weird."

It's heavenly, I think, keeping my pride to myself this time.

David left the table for a moment and returned with a photograph of me at about eighteen.

"Look at this. No wonder the boys were after her!" his voice was full of love. "Margie was part of the sixties. Me, I was part of the drug scene. The prescription drug scene!"

Everything was funny, even his jokes that I've heard so

many times before. There was no room for my analytical self, no room to self analyze. Not today.

I felt God's presence along with Mom, Dad and Doug. They were all at that table with us. I am so lucky, I thought, for the hundredth time that day.

"I should tell you about our niece, Jessie," David continued his joking, "She lives in Toronto and dates only b's and c's."

"David!"

"It's okay, they'll get a kick out of it." He waved me away and continued. "She dates bouncers. cops, ball players, construction workers. I keep telling her to move up in the alphabet. You know to d's. Doctors, developers, dentists."

Gradually, we all started to relax.

"Peter, do you golf?" David asked.

"No."

"Hurrah," I smiled at Peter, "a man after my own heart! I knew there was a reason I liked this guy so much." Peter looked surprised at my reaction so I explained David's obsession with the sport drives me crazy. "He golfs five or six times a week."

“No,” David smiled, “That’s not true. Only three or four times.”

“Ya, right.” I laughed and touched her hand. “I tried golf and I wish I could like it but it’s boring. I’m the founder of WAG, Wives Against Golf! I always say, I wish he would look at me the way he does his Big Birtha club. I prefer to walk on the beach."

"Hey, why don't I take you out to the club to hit a few balls and let the gals go for a walk?" David asked Peter, determined that his new son-in-law would become a golfer.

CHAPTER 18

WE WENT FOR the first of many walks on the dike in Richmond. It formed a protective hill from the marshy flats which spread out for a mile offshore. We passed million dollar homes along the Fraser River. The airport was on the other side and Cassandra pointed out each plane as it landed. Simple events were made exciting in the enthusiasm of a baby's discovery.

We continued on past marshlands and a bird sanctuary. We saw cows grazing on a farm pasture. We both started mooing as we pointed them out to Cassandra. A seaplane flew overhead.

Never before had I had anyone so interested in me. Every word was dispersed with massive giggles, like two teenage girls discussing their boyfriends, every exchange was a wondrous discovery of each other.

We walked back to the car at that magical hour just before sunset when the shadows were long and everything was pronounced, soft pink hues, the mountains and ocean. It felt as though we were walking inside a painting.

"Are you mad at me for giving you up?" I asked.

She stopped. She looked surprised at my question. "No, of course not. I love my parents."

"I realize that, but do you feel any resentment that I have had such a good life?"

"I'm glad you did." Linda stopped to face me, "So did I."

OVER DINNER THAT night, at Umberto's, a popular Tuscan restaurant, I announced, "I have a gift for you."

"I have one for you, too," Linda said.

"Wouldn't it be funny if you both gave each other the same thing," Peter pitched in.

I took the small gift from my purse. It was the most precious thing I could offer - the gold locket my mother had given to me the day she died. "It was a gift to my mother from her mother when she graduated from the University of Toronto."

"I graduated from U of T also," Linda said when she opened it.

"It seems fitting that I carry on the tradition and give it to my daughter," I said. I needed to feel that I passed on something

of myself and my family to her.

Shyly, she pulled a small box from her pocket. "Peter was right." I opened the box and discovered a gold locket. "It has a picture of Cassandra in it and I thought you could put the picture of your next grandchild on the other side."

"I shall cherish it always," I said getting up from the table to hug her yet again and smell her hair and feel the warmth of her embrace.

"Cool," said Peter proud that he had predicted the gifts properly. I opened the locket and kissed the picture of my granddaughter.

After dinner, back at the house, I changed my first diaper. What a pleasure. Another first in my life as a grandmother. I curled up on the couch with Noel to watch our wedding video.

"That's my dad." I pointed to the screen. "He was so frail. David said in his speech that he thought they'd have to play the song twice so Dad could make it down the aisle! I never danced with my father at our wedding. I will never forgive myself for that. I wish someone had mentioned it to me. I was so nervous. I forgot. I still feel guilty."

“Mmm,” Noel touched my hand sympathetically.

“We walked to a hymn my mother published when she was fourteen.” Noel, no, Linda nodded her head. She was a great audience, totally absorbed in my story.

“Our first dance was to Barbara Streisand singing, 'What are you doing the rest of your life.' We listen to it every anniversary and watch this video.” I glanced towards my husband. “I wondered for years if I was capable of loving anyone enough to want to sing that song to him.” David winked. “Did I tell you that David proposed to me on my parents' anniversary?" The words poured out of my mouth.

I wish my parents could be here now. Perhaps they were. And Doug. In this very room watching us on another dimension, influencing our reunion.

I turned to my daughter and said, "David gave a great speech."

"I want to hear it," Linda said.

"You will. It's coming soon."

"Peter messed up his speech at our wedding."

"Hey," said Peter lowering the video camera for a

moment. "Watch it." More giggles. The camera continued to record us. Linda pulled a face. She looked crossed eyed into the lens which I soon learned was her trademark.

"There's Jeannette, a friend of mine," I said, pointing back at our wedding video. "You'll meet her tomorrow. She can't wait. I wouldn't let her come today. I wanted you all to myself. Selfish, eh? The day Charlotte faxed your picture to my office, she rushed over to see it."

Linda was patient as I named each guest. "My friend Lori can't believe I kept you secret from everyone all these years.

Toward the end, she called out, "Wait! Go back a bit." I looked at her, puzzled, but rewound the tape. "Stop. Freeze that frame." Linda pointed to my leg on the chair as David was removing my garter. "I don't believe it." Linda looked at me, "I wore the same shoes at my wedding."

Peter laughed. "Wow, same gift and same shoes. That's amazing."

It was more than amazing. I looked at my daughter's smiling face and once again felt my entire life validated in our similarities.

After the wedding video, we poured over photograph albums for hours. I made her look at every picture I had of my mother and my father, Doug, Jeff and all our relatives, trying to give her a sense of her ancestry.

"There's a photo of your paternal, great, grandmother. She was born in Virginia during the Civil War. Back then, I understand if there wasn't a lot of money, it was common practice for the wives to follow their husbands into war. Your great, great grandmother was pregnant and gave birth right on the battlefields so they named their daughter Virginia. Your Uncle Jeff and his wife are trying to get pregnant and if they have a girl, they plan to call her Virginia after her."

"Neat," Linda said. "I considered calling Cassandra Noel," she paused and touched my hand, "but decided it would hurt my parents."

Smiling, I turned the page, "There's my cousin Rosemary. She adopted a daughter after you were born. A little blonde baby, Ann. I immediately asked her birth date. I wanted her to be you. Every baby I saw made me yearn for you. I observed other children in order to keep track of how you might look at

various ages."

Linda appeared pleased.

"Jeff had a girlfriend once who was adopted. She was blonde and the right age. I worried sick until I met her and realized that my brother wasn't dating his niece. Every girl I saw became you. I searched the faces of blonde children to find you there."

"Thing's are so different now. Lots of teenage girls keep their babies."

"Yes," I agreed sadly. "Morals change. Despite the so-called rebellion of the sixties, it was very difficult to be independent. If you had been born a few years later, things might have turned out differently." I paused and pondered the idea.

"Do you have a picture of my father?" Noel asked timidly.

I lowered the photo album and looked at her anxious face. "No, I don't." I patted her arm. "I'm sorry. I burned most pictures of my teenage years."

Hours passed as we sat, photo albums spread out over the floor, Cassandra crawling among them.

"I'm seventeen here."

Linda jumped up and left the room, returning with photographs of herself. "Where's that picture of you at seventeen?" She handed me the one of herself. "Our smiles are the same, a little crooked."

"Leaning Tower of Pisa smiles, I call them. My brothers are the same." I pointed at another photo, then at her face. "Your bangs are cut and I have on too much make-up but you can see the similarities here too."

"Yeah." Linda agreed.

"Wait a minute!" I jumped up. "I have a family tree that my father printed. I'll get you one." I ran to the bookcase and took a copy out, carefully opening it to my family. "I have to do something before I give it to you." Taking a pen, she watched as I wrote her name and Cassandra's into my father's family tree. "I never liked this book because I always knew it was a lie," I said as I handed it to her. The pain of twenty-seven years vanished with adding her name under my entry in the family tree. Smiling at Peter, I said into the video camera, "Who could ask for more?"

Finally, Peter wondered out loud if I would ever let them

go back to their hotel room. He had insisted that they stay in a hotel so they could spend some time on their own to relax from all the excitement.

I MADE DAVID stay up another hour after they left, dissecting her every move, her every gesture. As I took off my makeup, I thought I looked at least twenty years younger. The secrets of the past, the guilt, shed like a reptile's outer skin, leaving the insides exposed and soft. A new identity looked back at me, that of Mother and Grandmother.

"What did I do that was so right to deserve this?" I asked David. "I must have pleased the gods in some way to be given this treasure."

David sat on the edge of the bed in his pajamas. "I love you this happy."

"I love being this happy," I kissed him. "You know what I think?"

He shook his head, "No, what do you think?"

"I think life is like the stock market. Life is full of cycles with everything having it's own turn to shine."

“Yeah, so?”

“So, this is my time. The bull market of my life. "

CHAPTER 19

APRIL FOOLS DAY! And the joke was on life. We tricked it, Linda and I, turning my deepest secret into bliss! We went to the country club to watch Yael play tennis. Peter joined us with his video camera in hand to film Yael playing. Her impish smile revealed how much she enjoyed the attention.

Then, as The First Lady of Joy, I gathered my new little family together and set off to show them my Vancouver.

We went to Chinatown for a breakfast of Chinese buns in the tea room behind the Leung Fong Bakery where I always felt as though I had stepped into the back streets of Hong Kong. Linda seemed to enjoy stepping out of a common territory to explore different cultures that I had discovered during my travels. I introduced her to long buns filled with coconut, barbecued pork buns, custard tarts and red bean paste sesame balls, still hot as the waiters passed us on aluminum trays. All the while, we shared our table with a toothless old man who smiled at us from behind his Chinese newspaper. I promised we would come to Chinatown another time for dim sum.

She laughed as I planned our future. Constantly re-assuring myself that there would be other times together. Our future. A time for us.

Next, we ventured off to Granville Island to walk the seawall. Vancouver gave its best for her. The sun shone. Sailboats and motorboats graced the water as they ventured out from their moorings on this perfect spring day. I was grateful it didn't rain. I pointed to each picturesque view as though I had created it just for her. We passed the houseboats which created a community all its own. I told her about some of the eccentric inhabitants who lived there, Doctor Tomorrow, the futurist and Stanley Burke, a political cartoonist. I held her as we walked. I needed to touch her. I pushed Cassandra in the stroller, Peter following with his video camera.

Linda stopped in front of a rose colored rhododendron bush and asked Peter, "Take some footage with the blossoms behind us," then added, "I know we look better than the flowers though."

I knew I would pause and smile every time I walked here after this day.

I never referred to Linda as Noel out loud, but in my heart, that would always be my name for her. Would I ever get used to Linda, I wondered, as I observed her in jeans and a light wind breaker, her blonde hair blowing in the breeze. We posed for more pictures, arm in arm.

"Don't film our behinds," Linda said to Peter. We both instinctively covered our bottoms and giggled.

Peter stopped and asked, "What do you want to be called? Nana, Grandma or Something else?"

"I don't know. I haven't thought about it."

"What did you call your grandmother?" Linda asked.

"Gaga."

"Gaga!" She crossed her eyes. More giggles.

Shrugging, I replied, "Doug started it. He didn't know how to say grandma. I just used my big brother's name for her." My hands moved up and down nervously on Cassandra's carriage. Picking my name felt like a big decision.

"Well, we have an Oma and we have a Grandma, so..." Peter speculated.

"I don't feel like a Gaga. My grandmother was really

old."

"It's up to you." Linda said.

"I'll have to think about it some more."

"Stay tuned. We'll have an answer later." Linda laughed into the video camera.

“I know!” They waited. “I know what I want to be called.”

“What?”

“Grandmama.” I announced. “I never got to be a mother so I’d like to be a GRAND Mama.”

“Grandmama, it is then.”

We ate lunch at Bridges. Its bright yellow exterior and huge deck overlooking the boats and the Burrard Street bridge made it one of Vancouver's most popular spots. Cassandra gave me my first kiss. A slobbery lick, really. I wiped it off and Linda scolded me, saying I shouldn't wipe off my granddaughter’s kiss. I rubbed it back on laughing. “I need to read the new Grandmother's handbook.”

After lunch, we crossed False Creek in the small battery powered ferry to the Aquatic Centre. A curious seal watched our passage. We walked along the seawall towards English Bay.

I counted eleven freighters anchored. Colorful kites flew in the sky, across the water, at the planetarium. Sailboats passed us, motoring as they made their way out of False Creek towards the open water.

"Vancouver is full of hardy souls," I said, pointing towards a wind surfer in a wetsuit. It was still a little cool for water sports. "I love that about this city. You can go sailing in the morning, golf or hike in the afternoon and ski on Grouse Mountain at night." I smiled proudly. "Because the markets here are tied to the New York markets, I feel as though I work in New York the morning, but when the markets close, I go home to the peace of Vancouver after the markets close at one o'clock. I sit on the beach and catch up by reading analysts' reports. Why sit indoors when I have this?" I asked her pointing towards the water, the sand and the mountains.

I stopped underneath my mother's tree. "This is where I come to talk to my Mom," I explained. "We were watching a movie of Vancouver when she died. The sun setting behind the mountains and English Bay, was the last thing she saw. I feel close to her when I sit here. I've said many a prayer about you

under this tree. Praying that you were happy, alive and well." Linda touched my hand tenderly. "I think sharing death with my mother is as spiritual a connection as sharing my birth with her and I have a similar connection to my father's death," I sighed and looked at Linda, "Did I tell you that he died where I was born?" She shook her head. "I assume Dad thought he had to go to the bathroom, just as my mother did the day I was born because he was found on the bathroom floor in the exact spot where I was born. Kind of spooky but comforting as well. Makes me feel very connected to them both to share in my birth and their deaths.

LATER, WE WANDERED through Granville Island Market, picking out fresh fruits and vegetables, pastries, shrimp, scallops and smoked salmon from the stalls. All Linda had to do was imply that she liked something and I bought it.

"Stop," she said, "you're spoiling us."

"I've waited for twenty-seven years to spoil you. Please let me."

ON THE THIRD day of my daughter's visit, we threw a party. As I prepared, Peter followed me around with his camera. It made me nervous to have him document my every move. When he asked for a beer, I quipped, "Get it yourself. I'm too busy to wait on you."

"Oh I see. Yesterday, we were guests and today we're family."

"And tomorrow David and I will put up our feet and let you wait on us!"

We invited my cousins, Robin and Rosemary, Yael and a few of our closest friends. Shiera called from university in Las Vegas. So did David's parents, to welcome Linda into the family.

Peter's aunt and uncle came over along with John who made our meeting possible with his approval. When Charlotte, Peter's aunt, came through the door, her mouth fell as she stared at me. "I know you! We've met!" She recalled the day about a year earlier when I came into her real estate office. I remembered the day well. It was just before we bought our house in Richmond and I had stopped to pick up a real estate guide of the area.

To think we were so close. What would I have done if she

said I looked just like her niece? Would I have questioned her? I don't think so unless she had told me that her niece was adopted. If only... Mustn't think like that. It was meant to happen now, not then. David used the Jewish word for it, 'bashert', meaning predestined.

The energy that night was emotional for everyone. The men told jokes to alleviate the nervousness. Cassandra, wide awake, loved a party even at eight months, coming by her party nature honestly, I thought proudly, as I observed Linda enjoying herself and felt my own face flushed with excitement.

Yael informed her new stepsister that I was a combination of several television characters: Diane on Cheers, Blair on Facts of Life and Rose of the Golden Girls. Apparently, one insult was not enough!

One friend, Joyce played my mother's piano. I had it shipped to Vancouver in 1980. None of the family played.
It broke my heart to see Mom's beautiful baby grand sit silent, year after year, so when Joyce sat down and played old fifties tunes and everyone stood around and sang, I thought back on the happier days of my childhood. Yael and Linda laughed at

some of the silly sentimental lyrics but they both knew the words and joined in wholeheartedly.

I kept glancing at the photo of my mother on her baby grand. I'm sure she was smiling as her piano came alive. I left the room and came back with a photo of my grandmother and placed it beside my mother's photo and pointed out how much the four of us looked alike. Everyone agreed. Their comments charged me like an Eveready™ battery. Linda blushed with the constant attention.

Noticing her blush, I said, "You must feel like a science experiment, the way everyone is dissecting you."

"Sort of, but I guess it's to be expected. You'll get the same treatment when you visit us in Toronto," she smiled. What joy, she just assumed I would visit.

I looked forward to the day when she will first complain about me. I long to be called 'Mother' even a long drawn out 'Oh MOTHeeeeer!'

Our children help to define who we are. I had never experienced that before. In the past, I would find my attention drifting off if someone bragged about their child too long,

showing me photographs and relaying their latest accomplishments.

For years I felt isolated, separated from society, as if I didn't belong. Even after I married, the feeling persisted. David and his daughters were cast from the same mold. They were blood relatives, Jewish and great tennis players. I was the outsider.

What makes a family? Do we owe something to the people who raised us or do they need to earn our love? Where do the bonds and obligations begin and end?

I haven't earned Linda's love, the right to be her mother, to participate in her life, but we have a clean slate on which to build our relationship. It's an advantage in some ways.

It validated me and I believe she felt the same. Linda had told me earlier that day that all of her life, her parents had told her to 'settle down, 'don't wear your heart on your sleeve'. They were very reserved in comparison to her. In meeting me, she said, she finally understood why her personality was the way it was.

"Out of control!" I had responded, "Thanks a lot."

"Seriously," she confided," it helps me to feel more confident about who I am."

The party moved into the billiards room. I took the video camera from Peter and filmed Linda's reactions, jumping up and down, arms in the air when she sank a ball, her tummy protruding, face glowing, crossing her eyes into the camera lens.

"I love this machine!" I said holding the video camera towards Peter. "When you've missed twenty-seven years of someone's life, you want to capture these moments to cherish after you leave. It's amazing to think that future generations will not only know what their ancestors looked like but understand their personalities as well." Peter smiled at my enthusiasm. "I sure wish I had footage of my parents and Doug. It's so much better than old black and white photographs."

As their visit unfolded, I dared to dream of celebrating Christmas again. Of family outings and renting a summer cottage. I dreamed of the girls, my girls, Linda, Yael and Shiera bonding as sisters. Of family dinners all seated together on a Sunday evening. Of phone calls, just to say, 'Hi, I miss you.' Of a family, my family.

We all took turns singing with the Karoke machine. Yael and Linda sang *Lady in Red* to the wrong tune and off key, laughing together as though they had known each other for years.

At the sound of the next few bars on the Karoke machine, I stopped. It was the song I sang to my baby years ago at the foster mother's home. No longer depressed by the words, I approached my daughter, microphone in hand. Nervous, I turned to Yael and grabbed her hand, "Stay and help me."

"What song is this?" she asked.

"A very special song," I said then started to sing, the poignant words from West Side Story.

"There's a place for us, a time and place for us. Somewhere, somehow."

Linda smiling, at first, put her hand to her mouth as she realized the significance of what I was singing. Yael put her finger into her mouth as though throwing up, but all I cared about was my daughter. The noise in the room stopped while I sang to my daughter as I had twenty seven years ago in the foster mother's home. Linda wept as I sang to her.

"We'll find a new way of living. We'll find a way of

forgiving. Sometime, somehow. There's a place for us, a time and place for us."

Later, David explained there was a Yiddish word for what I was feeling. It is 'simcha' which means boundless joy.

Peter focused the video camera on Linda. She hid behind his uncle and allowed her tears to steam down her face. She hugged Cassandra close just as I had held her twenty-seven years earlier. My voice cracked with emotion but I continued to sing. I didn't care. Our sometime was now. We would find a new way of living and I was forgiven, in her acceptance of me. As the song ended there was silence.

Her Uncle Hans laughed to break the ice. "I'm sure glad Linda found you," he announced, looking at me, then at David. "We're all tired of supporting her. Now, it's your turn." The magical moment lapsed as everyone laughed.

OUR GUESTS LEFT but I didn't want Linda, Peter and Cassandra to return to their hotel. I wasn't ready for the evening to end. Peter and David watched television. Linda and I lay sprawled on the living room floor, stroking Cassandra between

us. In response to her questions, I told her about the months I was hidden in my parents' basement, about the clinic for unwed mothers, her foster mother. I tried to play down my grief but those feelings, hidden for years, were ignited once again. Excitement passed over into sheer exhaustion and finally grief. The more my emotions surfaced, the more I realized how successful I had been at deadening them over the years. Tears involuntarily streaked my cheeks as I realized that meeting my daughter accentuated my loss in a way her absence never had.

Peter wandered in with his camera. "What's happening?"

"We're having a quiet moment," Linda said softly.

Peter pointed the camera at me.

"Please, I don't want to be emotional on film," I said, covering my face.

"I need something to show my friends where I got it from," Linda said.

"Why are you upset?" Peter asked from behind the camera.

"I've been watching Cassandra," my words choked. " It's just that I know now what I've missed."

"Reality just hit," Linda smiled at her husband.

"Oh, God, turn that thing off," I stood and put my hand in front of the camera.

My daughter lowered her head shyly and spoke with compassion, "Isn't she great?"

"It was much easier when he wasn't here," I said pointing to Peter.

"I can leave if you want."

"Yes, go away. No," I grabbed Peter's arm. "I want you to stay. If I let you keep running that thing, will you just not go home."

By two-thirty in the morning we were almost deliriously tired. Cassandra had been asleep for hours. David was in bed and Peter had dozed off in front of the television. Linda and I were still stretched out on the living room floor where the embers from the fire gave off a mystical light.

"I took French immersion one summer at the University of Montreal." Linda said.

"Really," I pushed up on my arms, "so did my brother!"

Linda sat up, "Oh my God, it's 2:30. I haven't been up

this late since..." she searched her memory, "since... since I got married!" Throwing her face back, hilarity spilled out between the words. "What does that tell you!"

"Me, neither." Punchy from lack of sleep, we couldn't stop laughing. We collapsed into each other, rolling on the floor, deep belly laughs rolled up in wave after wave. I would try to stop, but Linda would cross her eyes and I'd start laughing again, releasing the stored nervousness of the past month.

Finally, wiping away tears, Linda sat up. "That felt good. I haven't laughed so hard in ages and it wasn't even funny. If Peter's listening from the den, he'll think we're crazy."

"It made me hungry," I said, holding my side.

"Me too. I can't believe how much we've eaten today."

I laughed and said, "Tomorrow, I fast all day. Fast. Then we better eat some more tonight." I stood.

"I'll get the cake." Linda said.

"I'll mix the drinks." Looking at her protruding belly, I said, "A Caesar for me and a virgin one for you. "

CHAPTER 20

I CAN'T BELIEVE I told the people at work, but yesterday I relayed my most personal story, Pssst, like a hot stock tip. And it was a hot tip. The hottest of my life.

Now a small select group gathered in my office where they greeted Linda warmly. I stood with my arm around her, smiling proudly. Barry, who headed the compliance department, was teary eyed. He had lost his son in a tragic work accident the previous year. The boy was the same age as Linda. I had cried uncontrollably in church, remembering Doug and understanding Barry's loss. We connected on a soul level at the funeral and I wanted him to share in my new found happiness.

Connie from RSP's said she felt privileged to have me share my story. She told me about a friend of hers who was reunited with her son after twenty odd years and how the son was a drug addict who hit her up for money. Her friend felt so guilty about giving him up for adoption and having his life turn out badly that she secretly kept giving him money. When her husband found out, he divorced her.

Grace stood on the outside of the circle, observing. We often sat together in the lunch room. When I told her about my daughter the previous day, she informed me that she and her twin brother were adopted and that he had met their birth mother. Grace said she didn't want to meet her. I asked why and Grace said the woman lived on a reservation and was a whore who used adoption as a form of birth control. There were several siblings it seemed. I was shocked, but she assured me that she loved her adoptive parents and had no need to meet the woman who had so casually given birth to her and her brother. Now Grace smiled at Linda and said, "You are very lucky to find a mother like Margaret." My heart went out to her. I wanted to take her in my arms and claim her as my daughter as well.

Monica, my office mate, had watched me giggle for days now so I wanted to include her in my secret coming out. She was so excited for me, it was as though she had found a daughter also.

I had been extremely sensitive about whom I shared Linda with but when we left my office, I bumped into a broker I barely knew and blurted, "This is my daughter. I gave her up for adoption and I've just found her. We were reunited this week."

The woman looked confused and stopped to digest the information. When she realized what I was telling her, she started to ask a question, but embarrassed, I quickly turned away. So much for not telling everyone. I felt a red flush rise up my neck like a tidal wave after a tsunami.

"YOU WOULDN'T BELIEVE it," I laughed after telling David about the positive reaction from my co-workers.

"And why wouldn't it be positive?"

"I still get nervous telling people."

"Everyone I've told has been thrilled." David said.

"Who have you told? My God, I hope you're not going around telling everyone!"

"I've told a few friends. Don't worry, they're happy for you."

"Jesus, David, please consult me before you say anything."

"Why are you so uptight about it?"

"This is my life we're talking about. It's very personal, I don't want something so precious turned into cheap gossip."

He stood, leaned over me and held my head against his

hip. "Let them gossip."

"Please, don't go around telling people."

I curled my arms around his thigh and looked up at him. "I want to choose who knows."

"The girls and I are happy for you. That's all that should count."

"You don't care what people think, do you?"

"No. I could give a shit."

"I'm so lucky to have your support. Thanks."

David pulled the hair from my face.

I smiled suddenly. "I feel as though my life before this was just a dream and today I woke up."

David kissed me tenderly and said, "You are my sleeping beauty."

CHAPTER 21

THE LAST NIGHT of their stay, Linda, Peter and Cassandra moved into our home. With them in the next room, I couldn't sleep and fought the urge to sneak in and watch her sleep. In the morning, as soon as I heard them stirring, I arrived in their room with hot coffee.

"Café au lait."

"Hey, service in bed. I like that," Peter said.

"It's my honor." I said placing their coffees on the side table, proud that I now knew how my daughter took hers. " I intend to spoil you rotten every time you honor me with a visit and I'll do whatever it takes to get you back here real soon."

After our breakfast of blueberry pancakes, Linda and I took Cassandra for a walk along the dike.

Linda described her pregnancy with Cassandra and the day she was born, June 30th of the previous year. As my daughter spoke, the realization hit me. Linda went into labor on the same day that David and I had a major fight. It was the only time in our marriage that things had gotten that bad between us.

"Oh my God, that explains it."

Linda looked confused, "What are you talking about?"

"I went through labor with you!" I said. As we walked, I told her the story. I knew that I was depressed about not getting pregnant but for some reason it really hit me the same day Linda went into labor with Cassandra. I remembered the date because it was the July 1st holiday long weekend.

Poor David couldn't do anything right and I stomped out in a rage over some stupid issue and slept over at a girlfriend's apartment. I was no longer taking the fertility pills which had made me so mentally undone, so couldn't understand why I was so distraught.

"I obviously felt your labor. It's a surreal bond which transcended time, distance and even knowing you."

"Cool," Linda went on, "I registered to find you after I left the hospital."

"Last July?"

"Yes."

"That's when I asked to be referred to a psychiatrist!"

"A psychiatrist?"

Panic crossed her face, which I interpreted as, 'Is my mother a nutcase?' I quickly wanted to reassure her. "Being sterile really threw me for a loop. I expected to get pregnant easily. I prayed every day for a baby boy. I didn't want a girl. I could never replace you."

Her hands caressed her protruding belly. "I want you to come to Toronto when I deliver."

"Could I?" My excitement showed. "How would Peter feel with me in there?"

"Not in the delivery room," her hands flew to her cheeks. "I couldn't handle that. I just meant to visit me."

"Oh," I said, hiding my disappointment.

IT WAS TIME to say goodbye.

At the airport, Linda cried uncontrollably. Having suppressed my emotions for so many years, I didn't cry but felt her leaving with every fiber of my being. I was afraid to say goodbye and hugged her as I had twenty-seven years previously.

Following them to the departure gate, I tried to herd Linda, Peter and Cassandra in my arms all together trying to

prolong their departure. Thanking her constantly for coming. Rambling gibberish, I raked my brain for ideas to keep them close.

Peter pulled free, glanced at Linda and pointed at his watch. I stood holding her hand and saw her return his look with an expression which indicated, *what can I do? She won't let go.*

"When can you come again? Can I visit you?"

"Mother's Day would be nice."

"Mother's Day! My first!" Satisfied, I released her to the skies that would carry her home, three thousand miles from me.

I would quit my job, I mused. Move. Buy a little house in Milton and play Grandmama for the rest of my days. But David would never move East and leave his daughters. He loved Vancouver and his law practice was not transportable. If I wasn't married, I have no doubt of where I would be: close to my daughter.

I stayed at the gate watching her as long as I could, waving and blowing kisses. Then, she disappeared.

Linda telephoned when they arrived back home. "I could see the dike we walked on when the plane took off and I started to cry. I miss you already."

She missed me! Boy, that felt good.

CHAPTER 22

April 5,1993

Dear Linda-Noel,

Linda, Noel, Linda, Noel, I struggle so much with What to call you. Noel, whom I longed for. Noel, whom I want to bundle up close to me and never let go.

Noel, whom I have mourned for and longed for and loved so sadly for so long and whom I now can't believe is really here. I want to cry out your name, my name for you, over and over and over. I want to hear it spoken aloud after all these years of hiding it, never uttering it to anyone.

It means so much to me that you have known your name all along. I must thank your parents when I meet them. I never thought you knew of me and certainly never thought you knew your name. I treasure knowing that you have thought of me over the years.

Yes, I want to call you Noel and yet I feel so awkward with it. It is still a secret between us. I still feel shame. I have not earned the right to use this precious name aloud.

Then there is Linda. The beautiful, perfect Linda of today. The Linda I hold in awe. The Linda I want to hold but with outstretched arms, at a distance, just to get a good look at her. Linda, the woman. The mature, giving, loving woman who has walked into my life holding her greatest treasure, Cassandra, my granddaughter, as a gift saying, "I want to share. I want to make up for your sadness." Linda the woman who I also want to bundle up close to me and make her Noel.

When I think of you as Linda, you are more manageable. I think of you as shared with your dear parents who kept me in your life, who are so generous in their gift as you are with Cassandra. What could I do for them to show the magnitude of my thanks? I have waves of gratitude wash over me when I think of how great is the gift of Noel and Linda. Linda. Noel. I love them both for different reasons and the same. Linda is the reality. Noel is the dream. Linda is the cake. Cassandra and Peter are the icing. And I get to have it all. This is life at its fullest.

Love,
forever and ever,
M

SEVERAL WEEKS HAD passed since their visit and I continued to telephone her every day but knew I must stop pestering her. She was busy with her own life, but I wasn't ready just yet.

The few friends I had confided in, honored my secret. I couldn't go completely public yet, partly from the residual shame, although every day the pain eased and I healed a little more. Linda's acceptance aided the cure.

I glanced at the array of congratulation cards on display. Everyone had been kind. Doug's son, James, sent me a touching letter about finding family, reminding me he grew up without his father. I often thought of Doug. He would be thrilled about Linda.

AFTER THEY RETURNED home, Peter spent hours, putting photographs of Linda's childhood on video. Appropriately, he set the scenes to the tune of Fleetwood Mac's 'Don't stop thinking about tomorrow.'

I settled into the couch with Cleo purring on my lap and watched her life flash by: Linda at two on a swing, blowing out her fifth birthday candles surrounded by friends I'd never met, playing ball at age ten, dress up parties, her pet German Shepherd and, of course, the parents who raised her.

Watching the video, it appeared that she was happy with her adoptive family. A cute child dressed as a tomboy, blonde hair cropped short, holding a pan to feed the squirrels at the summer cottage. Her image stared at me from the video and my heart tightened. Finally, my tears fell.

David walked in and held me. He wanted to make it better but how could he? No one could.

"But you have her now. Be grateful." He tried to console me.

"I know and I am grateful but tonight I need to mourn."

Quietly, he rocked me, "There's an old Hebrew fable," David related as I collapsed exhausted onto his lap.

"There was a woman at the beach with her baby. It Was a lonely beach far from civilization. Suddenly a large wave washed her baby out to sea. Not being able to swim and with no help for miles, the woman turned her hands to the heavens and prayed. 'Please, dear God, bring my baby back safely'. She prayed and prayed, beseeching God to return her baby. She was a religious woman and believed her constant prayers would be answered. Suddenly a large wave flowed to shore and sure enough there was her baby safe and sound. She grabbed her baby and turned to the heavens, and said, 'Hey, he had a hat!'"

He waited, letting his words sink in. Hearing my soft chuckle, he said, "Don't dwell on what you don't have. I know losing her childhood is not like a hat, but focus on the fact that she has been returned to you safe and sound."

"It isn't that easy."

"I know, honey, but you must settle for the life you have."

“I have a great life. Guess I feel guilty.” David held me until my tears were exhausted. “I so wanted us to have a baby.”

“I’m sorry too. He would be three now.” It was the first time David had expressed any disappointment.

“She saved me, you know, and she saved us."

"What do you mean?" he asked.

"I wouldn't ever have gotten over not having our Samuel Douglas. If I hadn't found her now, I'm not sure our marriage could have withstood it."

"Sure it would. We love each other. Don't talk like that."

April 8,1993

Dearest Linda-Noel,

Do you know that you are almost constantly in my thoughts? I keep re-running our week together and I smile. I remember special moments, a look on your face, a smile, your laugh. And I smile. People must wonder about me as I smile to myself - lost in my happy reality.

I remember bits of conversations and wish we could talk longer. I think I must ask more about that. This and that of your life.

I wander around the house and picture you snuggled up on the couch in our family room, laughing, singing with Yael, playing pool. Ordinary events made special by your presence.

I remade your bed today and I hugged the pillow and thought, 'my Noel slept here'. I feel your presence in my home and I smile.

I carry your flowers from room to room with me. Twenty-seven flowers for twenty-seven years. So thoughtful. Last night I placed them in the den as I watched the video of our week together. I have them now in the breakfast nook as I write to you. I wake up to their scent beside my bed.

My heart is so full of everything that is happening to me.

I put down my pen and sipped my glass of wine. I had opened a bottle of Beaujolais Nouveau and put out a plate of crackers with Brie and Gorgonzola cheese. Spirited Latin music gave me a festive feeling as I wrote. I picked up my pen and continued,

Finding you is very physical for me. I feel I have found that part of my soul, my essence that was missing. I feel I want to gather up your energy and bring it back to me. That is why I keep touching you.

I know it embarrasses you but I can't help myself. I need to reinforce that you are real. But primarily, it is to gather your energy back so that I can feel whole again. I want to hold you as close as I can, to feel you in my arms and envelope you in my love. To leave my mark on you, staking my territory like an old mother cat.

Heaps and heaps of love, M

I HAD JUST finished bringing my daughter's flowers down from the bedroom and had set them on the kitchen counter. I

was enjoying the warmth of the sun through the window, heating my body when the phone rang and took me out of my reverie. He phoned out of the blue.

How strange it was for Paul, my first boyfriend, to show up after all these years. Especially now. He was in Vancouver on a holiday and asked me to meet him for coffee in Steveston. I drove to the small fishing village and parked. He was sitting at an outdoor cafe. I hadn't seen him since my own father's funeral five years ago.

He was no longer the Greek God who took my virginity. He was skinny, with a scrawny gray pony tail hanging down his back, An earring! I wondered how I had ever found him so utterly attractive.

The family I had envied for their closeness, he told me, had fought and divided after his mother died. He quit the family business and nothing had worked out for him financially since. He spoke of his divorce and the disappointment he felt in never having children.

"I should have married you," he said finally.

There was no joy in his confession. It had happened so

long ago and I'd moved on. Apparently, he hadn't and it amazed me he still thought about me at all and especially in those terms.

"Yes, Paul, you should have. I loved you very much back in the sixties."

"Are you happy?" His sad eyes held a glimmer of hope.

"Yes. I married a great guy."

"Too bad." His smile faint.

I pulled out my photo album of Linda and told him about our recent reunion. He gazed at her pictures longingly.

“Am I her father?” His eyes searched mine.

Shocked, I answered, "No.”

His eyes dropped. "I always wondered." He appeared truly disappointed.

“Why didn’t you ask?” Astonished he had thought my baby was his all these years and yet he had never asked me.

He shrugged, “I guess back then I didn’t want to know. Now, never having had children, I wish she were mine.”

I touched his hand, “Sorry."

I watched sadly as he drove away on his motorcycle.

CHAPTER 23

I SWORE THE day I left Juvenile Court, giving my baby to a stranger, I would never allow anyone hurt me again. But now it came from the one person who could hurt me most. My brother.

"I told Monica," Jeff said on the phone.

"And?"

"She didn't take it well."

"What do you mean? What's not to take well?"

"She's upset."

"What on earth does she have to be upset about?"

"She feels it's wrong. That it isn't something you should be proud of, a child born out of wedlock."

"What is she? Out of the middle ages?"

"Calm down. I'll work on her. She'll come round but in the meantime, I don't think you should visit us when you come on Mother's Day. Perhaps I could meet you and Linda for lunch at my office."

After I hung up, my anger festered. Quietly at first, Like a small shock from pulling out an electrical cord, but as the day went on, it grew. *How dare she! What kind of a prude was she? She slept with my brother for years before they married. How dare she sit in judgment of my life? She knew nothing of the circumstances. Had she had an abortion? Is that why she reacted so violently? There was no birth control when I got pregnant. No abortions. Thank god*, I thought.

I punched one hand into the other. I'll never set foot in her house again. I will NOT be judged by that woman. The old rage consumed me. Rage, not just at Monica, but at anyone who had hurt or judged me.

This was the most joyful time of my life and Monica was diminishing it. Surely, Jeff would side with me. Our years together had created a bond that couldn't be destroyed. He was my brother, my friend and I had raised him like my own son. Surely he would do what was right.

"HOW COULD YOU do that to me?" Jeff yelled into the phone a few weeks later.

"Do what?" I asked, confused.

"Our anniversary present," he said flatly.

"What about it?"

"You put Linda, Peter and Cassandra's name on the card."

"Yes and David, Shiera, Yael's. So what? I write that on all of my cards these days."

"You know Monica is upset."

"I did it because that is what I do now. I love them and want to acknowledge them as part of my family." I paused. "They are, you know, whether Monica likes it or not."

"Listen, I didn't tell you just how badly she is taking all this. I didn't want to hurt you but you mustn't do things like that. She was so pissed off, she threw the gift out."

"She threw my gift out! I don't believe it. Because I signed the card from my family? Which is your family. Her family, for God's sake. That's sick."

"She's not sick. She's entitled to her opinion. Do you want to destroy my marriage? I know you hate her!"

"Firstly, Jeff, I am not trying to destroy your marriage.

If you two are having some trouble it has nothing to do with me. I'm just happy to have found my daughter. I feel rewarded and privileged. The fact that I had a baby in the sixties also has nothing to do with your wife." I started to pace. "Secondly, I don't hate her but I've never felt comfortable with her. What's her problem?"

"She'll leave me if you push Linda on her."

"How do you feel about it? Do you think it's a disgrace that I had a baby?" My breath stopped. "Do you feel I'm bad or wrong in some way? "

"Of course not. I'm happy for you. But I must obey my wife."

"What are you telling me?"

"I can't allow you to bring your daughter here. You have to come by yourself when you visit."

"Linda is innocent. If Monica needs to be upset at someone, it should be me. My daughter is the victim here. Why would Monica reject her?" I paced the den, phone in hand, waving my free hand as I talked. "She has no right act superior. It's not acceptable."

"Monica has an old soul." Jeff offered as his explanation.

Throwing my head back, I asked, "What the hell does that mean? She's from the dark ages? This isn't Victorian times."

"We are old souls together. We go back a long way."

"Bullshit. No one else feels that way about my daughter. Everyone has celebrated with us. Even David's parents. If anyone should have a problem, it should be them. They're orthodox and in their seventies, yet they've taken in Linda like a new granddaughter. You! I can't believe."

"I'll talk to Monica. She'll come round. Let me handle it. Just don't ever do anything like that card again. And don't bring her when you visit. Come by yourself."

Suddenly, my daughter was no longer a miraculous find but had become an object, a 'no name her'. "You want me to visit and pretend my daughter doesn't exist?"

"I don't want you to mention her name to Monica, ever!"

"You of all people. I thought you loved me. I thought we were friends?"

"I do love you, but I love my wife. These are the terms

or you are not to come to our home again."

"I won't, not under those terms."

"Then we'll have lunch at my office."

"I don't understand why you're reacting this way? What about Linda? You were so anxious to meet her. Don't you want to anymore?" I didn't wait for his response. The rage, buried twenty-seven years ago, surfaced. "I can't talk to you any more. I'll call you later." I hung up.

DAVID COULD NOT console me. The more I cried, the angrier he became. "How could your brother behave this way? Linda owes you nothing but Jeff is a real disappointment after all you've done for him. I'm not surprised by that bitch. I've never liked her. With her judgmental smirk. Fuck them! Forget them!"

"You don't understand. How would you feel if your girls rejected you? I raised Jeff. I love him! I can't just turn it off."

"He's not worth it. You've done nothing but loved him." David rested his arm on mine.

Shaking his arm away, I screamed, "I can't just forget him!"

I turned away from my husband. I expected him to understand. Spinning around, I glared at David, "It hurts so bad." Gasping for air, I began hyper-ventilating.

"Stop crying," David demanded. "They're not worth it."

"You think I can stop!" I yelled at him between desperate gasps for air. "You've never lost anyone. You don't understand. I've lost everyone in some way or another! Now I've lost my kid brother. It almost hurts more than anything back in the sixties."

But as much as I prayed otherwise, even the mention of my brother brought forth a surge of tears.

A FEW DAYS later, David handed me a book. It was called, No Time To Mourn. "It's written by a friend of mine." He slipped his arm around my shoulder and led me to sit down on the couch. "I know you've had a tough time, our own personal dramas are painful, but I think you need to put it all in perspective. This guy makes your life look like a picnic. I think you should read it."

"I will."

And I did. It was a tragic account of Leon Kahn's life as a Holocaust survivor. He had fled his village in Lithuania in 1941 with his sister, brother and father when the Germans invaded. His mother refused to join them and stayed behind to nurse her sick mother. He never saw her again. He watched from the forest as hundreds of Jewish women were raped, murdered and thrown into a mass grave. He joined a resistance group, which ran attacks on the Germans. His sister was bayoneted in front of him. His father died in his arms of gunshot wounds and his brother was killed in an ambush. He lost a total of twenty-nine close relatives during the war. Afterwards, he moved to Vancouver, married and started a successful developing business and was known for his philanthropy.

How could anyone recover from such tragedies? My husband was a wise man. My sorrows were nothing in comparison to his friend. The human ability to endure and be able to laugh again, despite how much torture, is amazing. If Leon Kahn could move on, then so could I.

CHAPTER 24

"DAD TOLD ME about your brother," Yael said as nudged into me, demanding to be hugged.

"He shouldn't have told you. I asked him not to." I put my arm around her.

"You know there's no such thing as privacy in this family. I just wanted you to know how bad I feel for you," she leaned her head on my shoulder. "I'm sorry, Margs."

"Thank you, sweetie." ***I will not cry.***

"Listen, I know I can never be for you what Linda is but I just want you to know that I love you."

Her words caught me off guard. "What do you mean?"

"I know you miss Linda and that Shiera and I aren't your real daughters but we both love you very much."

I grabbed her shoulders, moving her away so I could see her face. "Oh, my God. You are the sweetest thing ever! You're right, you can never be for me what Linda is, but I

want you to know that she can never be for me what you are. Never! I've watched you and your sister grow up, for heaven's sake. I've shared your life, your most important passages of time. We've been together for celebrations, special events, holidays, quiet moments like this. Our history has bonded me to you in a way that I can never bond with Linda."

"Dad says you're upset because you haven't heard from her in awhile."

"God, does he tell you everything I say?" I pulled back, my face stern so she could understand how serious I was. "I spent twenty-seven years wondering where my daughter was. Now that I know, I don't want to miss a minute of her day, but she has a life, a little girl, she works, runs a home and she's pregnant. It would be unrealistic for me to think she has time to speak to me every day. I have to restrain myself from calling her constantly. I don't want her to roll her eyes when the phone rings because it's me again. I don't ever want to become that person."

"It's not normal," Yael agreed.

"If you or your sister didn't call, I would pick up the phone and give you heck. I would yell and scream, lay guilt trips, demand attention. My relationship with Linda is new and fragile. Can you appreciate the difference?"

"I guess." Yael's tears wet my skin as she leaned into me.

"Never doubt how special you are and how much I love you."

LINDA CALLED THE next day to confirm my plans for Mother's Day. I gave her my arrival time, but didn't mention my conversation with my brother. I would take her aside when I got there and give her the condensed version. No point upsetting her with the details on the phone. She was expecting an enthusiastic hug from her new uncle which I now knew wasn't coming. I wanted to protect her.

Why couldn't life be perfect? Just for a little while? Why did I have to lose my brother to gain my daughter? Why couldn't I have it all? Why couldn't everyone I loved, love me back?

CHAPTER 25

AS THE PLANE descended into the Toronto airport, I thought could have parachuted down if it brought me to her faster.

As I rode the escalator to the baggage area, I could see her at the bottom of the stairs, holding Cassandra. She was jumping up and down enthusiastically. I fell in love with her all over again.

Finally, in her embrace, words poured out, some making sense, most nonsense. People passed and smiled. It's awhile since they've seen each other, they must think. Yes, twenty-seven years!

“Everyone's waiting to meet you." Linda said.

I must have looked confused. "Peter's family,” Linda explained. “No one could wait till Sunday. His entire family is at the house. They would've come to the airport but I wouldn't let them. I wanted you all to myself for a moment before they consumed you. Now you're going to see how I felt in Vancouver.

I hope you won't be too overwhelmed."

"I've waited all my life to be a part of your life."

"It'll wear off one day, I'm sure," my daughter replied.

"Never!"

"You'll find out about the real me. Get bored." She joked.

"You might get bored with me." I replied.

"Overwhelmed maybe, but never bored. It's keeping up with you that concerns me. You never run out of energy,"

"Adrenaline. I've been walking on air since we met. Jeannette says I look twenty years younger. I feel it."

On the drive to her home, I looked out the window as we passed farmyards and open fields. "I used to drive my dad on country roads near here and photograph scenes he would paint later. I'll give you one."

"That would be nice."

"The last time I saw Dad alive, I drove him all through the back roads but he found it quite tiring. He was eighty-four and quite fragile, so we stopped for a long lunch at Caledon Hills."

I studied my daughter's face as she concentrated on

the road, her hands gripping the steering wheel as we progressed in heavy traffic on the sixteen lane highway. "I wish he had lived just a few more years so you could have met him. You would have liked him. Most people did. We clashed when I was younger because we were so much alike," I laughed, "both stubborn and opinionated. But I've come to realize that the traits I like most about myself, all came from him, his love of travel, reading, different cultures." I paused, "Sorry, I'm rambling."

"No, I'm enjoying it."

She braked suddenly as the traffic slowed and the aroma of manure filled the car. "Ah, fresh country air, eh."

I smiled, lost in my memories. "Dad used to brag about camping with members of the Group of Seven. You know these famous Canadian artists, don't you?" She nodded so I continued, "Dad said Franz Johnson chose Dad's oil as the best painting done one particular weekend. It's possible. He was a young student and as accomplished artists, they were kind to him." With a pang of regret, I recognized that my father was a damn good artist and wished I'd been kinder.

We slowed and turned onto the James Snow Parkway into Milton. Linda smiled. "Our neighbourhood is wonderful. Even if I won the lottery, I wouldn't move. It's similar to where I grew up."

My heart tightened briefly at her remark.

"That's where I'll have the baby," Linda pointed to a hospital as we passed.

"How are you feeling?" I asked looking at her tummy pressed tight against the steering wheel. She was large for six months and I thought it would be wonderful if she had twins.

"The baby kicks a lot. I'll let you put your hand there next time and feel him."

"Him? I thought you didn't know what you were having?" I asked surprised.

"I don't. I want a boy but I'm afraid if I have one, Peter won't try again. I'd like to have three but he worries about money."

"I want you to produce a baseball team!"

Linda laughed as she pulled onto a side street lined with mature trees starting to bud. "We're here."

Two story brick houses were built tight together on small lots, almost looking as though they were attached. I knew immediately which home was hers by the crowd waving madly on her front lawn under a large maple. Several people, all talking at once, surrounded the car as Linda pulled in front of the rust colored garage door.

"Get ready for the madness."

Each person tried to be the first to hug me as I stepped out of the car.

I noticed a woman who stood aside, quietly waiting her turn. Cecile, Peter's mother, looked the matriarch while radiating a natural warmth. Brown hair, glasses, late fifties, her hands were callused, I discovered later, from working in her organic garden. She processed vegetables into baby food for her grandchildren. A perfect Oma - tough competition. But with Cecile, I quickly learned, one never needed to compete. We embraced.

"I'm so glad to meet you." Cecile said, then she leaned closer and whispered, "Linda needed you."

My daughter needed me. Simple words, yet full of love and understanding. "I needed her," I answered. Our eyes held

for a brief moment before I was whisked off to continue the introductions.

"I'm Horst, Peter's father." An older version of Peter approached and took my arm authoritatively. "Let's go inside and get comfortable. Come, come." He motioned to the others. "I have champagne to toast this momentous event."

Inside the door, there was a long hallway filled with family photographs. Mine was not among them of course but in time, I hoped to earn a spot.

Champagne glasses lined a wooden coffee table. Chairs from the dining room filled the living room where every seat was taken while several other members of the family stood, their faces glowing with excitement.

"This is Kunzelman." Horst picked up the bottle and popped the cork. "From his vineyard at Niagara-On-The-Lake. He's a friend of mine from the old country. He makes the best wine in Canada!" He filled the glasses. "Everyone take a glass. Let's toast to Linda and her mother."

"Cheers! Prosit! Hurrah" the group called out. "Welcome to the family."

One by one, people filed in throughout the evening. I relaxed in their warm welcome. They were good people, caring, friendly and supportive. Everyone of them appeared genuinely delighted to be part of our reunion.

"You have a wonderful family," I said.

"Yes," she touched my hand. "And now I have two mothers to love me. Three with Cecile. I'm spoiled all around. And three fathers with mine, David and Horst and I guess there's potential to meet my birth father so that would make four dads. If he's married, then another mother! Can you imagine if Cassandra and Mitchell had four sets of grandparents? Boy, would they get spoiled."

AFTER EVERYONE LEFT, Peter went to work on his computer in the family room.

"He's addicted to computers just like David is addicted to golf." Linda told me. "He takes them apart and rebuilds them just to see if he can do it." Her voice was full of pride. "He has three in the basement in various stages of repair. Once a mechanic, always a mechanic."

"I'm impressed, being computer illiterate." I said.

"Not only does he know how to rebuild them but he's software crazy too. You'd love what he's doing right now. He's on a chatline."

" I feel so stupid. What do you mean by chatline?"

"People log on the computer from all over the world and talk to each other. You type in your conversation. The best thing is that it's free. Denise from Brazil is most likely on there now. Her chat name is Itszu. I told her about our reunion. She wants us to visit her in Brazil."

"Hoorah. When do you want to go?"

"I can't now but perhaps after the baby is born."

"That would be great."

"I haven't told you my chat name, have I?" I shook my head. "You're going to love it." She smiled sheepishly, pausing for a moment before saying, "Noelle."

"Noel? You use Noel?"

"I spell it N.O.E.L.L.E. so it's clear that I'm a woman. I thought you might like it. If you buy a computer for home, Peter would fly out and set you up so we can talk on line."

"I'll get one immediately."

"What chat name will you use?"

Without hesitation, I said, "Noellesmom. Would you mind?"

"Not at all." The significance was imprinted on her smile.

THE NEXT DAY we were to meet my brother for lunch. Saturday was scheduled with my mother's brother and his wife, my only relatives still alive from her generation. Sunday was Mother's Day. We were spending it with Peter's family. Monday, we were to have dinner with Linda's parents. I was concerned that Linda was not spending Sunday with her mother but she assured me that they seldom celebrated special occasions on the actual day and getting together on Monday would be fine.

It was late but I knew I must warn my daughter about Jeff. It was only fair.

"I have to talk to you about my brother and his wife."

"What?" She looked concerned.

"There's a problem." I summarized Monica's reaction without emphasizing her cruelty.

"That's unbelievable. This is the nineties, for God's sake. I hope he doesn't agree with her!"

"I don't think so but he's respecting her wishes." I didn't mention my anniversary gift tossed, unopened, into the garbage.

"So, I'm not going to meet my uncle?" Her tone swelled with disappointment.

"He wants to meet you, but without Monica this time."

"I want to call her and give her hell."

"So do I, but Jeff begged me not to interfere. I just wanted to prepare you that his enthusiasm has been dampened by his wife's reaction."

"Shit." Her tears flowed instantly. "I should have met him right away. I wondered why he stopped calling." It tore me apart to see her upset. "I really wanted to be hugged by my uncle."

I ran my fingers over her soft cheek. "Well, it may not be that easy after all."

And it wasn't.

CHAPTER 26

I WOKE UP in Linda's home, in the downstairs den. She brought coffee and Cassandra to my bed. Not coffee and a croissant, but coffee and a granddaughter. Perfect. I sat up and Cassandra crawled into my arms. Several family photos sat on the ledge above the fireplace. A collage of pictures spanning her married life hung on the wall behind her.

It was five a.m. Vancouver time and I was still groggy from our late night talk, but content to lie back and experience a quiet family moment. We talked like normal people.

The new baby's room was freshly painted a neutral beige ready for a boy or a girl. Their large master bedroom had a king-sized bed and a sewing machine in the corner with a dress half finished. ***Hmm, my daughter knows how to sew.***

Outside her bedroom, I stopped. A framed wedding invitation hung on the wall. I read it astonished and called for her to join me.

"This is my wedding invitation." I pointed to the frame.

"What?" She looked at me not understanding.

"It's the same. We chose the same invitation!"

"Get out." She answered in disbelief.

"Yes," I put my arm around her and stood staring at the framed memento, yet another sign of our similarities.

"May I see your wedding pictures?" I asked.

For the next few hours, we poured over her photo albums and watched her wedding video. She and Peter got married only ten months after I married David.

"We could have had a double wedding!" I laughed.

Linda didn't respond. *How stupid of me. How would her parents have handled our reunion if I had been around to share that special moment?* Watching their image on the video screen, I felt jealous. If only, Linda would have met my Dad. She could have been my Maid of Honor. *Stop it*! I shook my head. *Stop it.*

LUNCH WITH MY brother was hell. We arrived at his office at noon. His secretary, Pearl, bubbled with enthusiasm and gave us flowers with a congratulations card.

Jeff remained in his office, on the phone, giving us a weak wave. His face was blotchy, his eyes red and his hands were shaking. Linda watched her new uncle intently. I motioned for him to hang up.

Finally, he came out, arms at his side, face tight. "Hello," his voice was strained.

I threw my arms around him. “This is your niece!” I pulled him closer. "Isn't she beautiful? And Linda, this is your Uncle Jeff, my darling little brother." I poked him in the tummy.

I tried not to notice the icy feeling descend when he failed to respond. An awkward silence ensued that remained over lunch.

The restaurant Jeff chose was very elegant with contemporary art on soft beige walls. There was a quiet hush to the place as white jacketed waiters moved between tables with silver trays of nouveau cuisine – elegantly displayed miniscule portions which left you hungry and wondering what you could snack on once you got home. Customers in suits leaned towards each other and spoke quietly, I imagined, of business deals. My brother treated us like new clients he was trying to impress. I

bounced Cassandra on my lap and babbled on, trying to ignore his cool reception.

Who was this person? Not the boy who sat on my lap years ago, the boy I sat up with at night when he was sick, not the young man I took everywhere. This was not the child who told me, "Boy am I lucky to have a sister like you."

After lunch, he stood and started to walk away without saying goodbye. "Hello." I grabbed his arm as he waved to the waiter for the bill. "Don't we get a good-bye hug?" I grabbed him and hugged him.

He gave me a forced hug and a patronizing pat on the back as though I were some ancient aunt. With a strained smile towards his new niece, my brother turned and walked away. My arms dropped to my side. Stunned, I didn't know what to say. Linda remained silent.

I felt the familiar Alaskan iceberg hit my heart as I watched him walk out of my life. It was as though I was sitting on that hard bench at Juvenile Court.

I understood why he did it. To keep the peace, just like Mom used to say. I knew he had enough capacity to love us all,

but apparently his wife didn't agree, so he was forced to make a choice.

I turned to the beautiful, sensitive woman beside me who looked equally horrified and said, "I need another drink."

At least I had an ally. We sat for another hour and dissected the situation, not arriving with any solutions but helping each other through the loss of a brother and an uncle.

CHAPTER 27

"MMMM, WHAT SMELLS so good?" I asked coming down the stairs.

"Roast. I made you a roast of pork," Linda called out from the kitchen.

"Wow, I haven't had pork for so long. Mom used to make it for me whenever I came home from a trip."

"I know. I remembered you telling me that on our first visit. That's why I did it," Linda said with that infectious smile of hers, shy, proud and full of love.

"You remembered! I forgot I told you," I said planting a kiss on her forehead.

I picked up a knife and started to peel potatoes. It was a simple act but I was acutely aware of the significance of mother and daughter preparing a meal together. Rich in the moment, I could feel the texture of the potato skin as I peeled, the cold water running over my hands as I washed them under the tap. I heard

the sound of children playing outside while my daughter set the table and Cassandra cooed from her place on the floor. The smell of the roast filled the kitchen.

SATURDAY WE VISITED my aunt and Mother's brother, Uncle Mort. He was the second youngest of the seven siblings and the last living relative of that generation. I was excited that Linda would meet him, explaining he was the most similar to my mother, somewhat shy and reserved, definitely a gentle soul. His wife was different from any of the women in my family. Uncle Mort always stood in the background, enjoying her ability to entertain with her outrageous humor, for as long as I could remember. Whenever I felt down, it was Aunt Marie I called to make me laugh.

My uncle told me that he always knew about my daughter but never mentioned it to anyone, honoring the family code of silence. But that day, he was genuinely excited to meet his great niece and hugged her tight with loving enthusiasm.

He had called the present owners and arranged for us to visit 191, the family code name for the home my mother grew up

in. I'd never been inside since it was sold before I was born.

Still I remembered my mother's stories of singing around the piano, Friday night dinners served by their Finnish servants. I had lived with these stories all of my life and now I would finally enter her sacred ground. Mom had built it up so much, how could it have been anything but disappointing?

The rooms were smaller and plainer than I had imagined. The entry wasn't so grand. I expected a huge staircase where my mother and her sisters glided down wearing Gone With the Wind evening gowns. The small living room held a television in the corner where I envisioned my mother's piano used to sit.

The room that had been my mother's bedroom captured my imagination. Looking out the window she had looked out of as a child, I felt her presence and lingered a few more minutes while the current owner continued his tour of the house. A plump little girl with blonde hair and big blue eyes that sparkled with mischief, my mother was spoiled by an adoring family and servants. She used to mention the servants with such love in her voice, never in a pretentious way but with a dreamy look of longing. Remembering another time, another life.

She kept a pony in the yard and would climb down the tree outside her bedroom window at night to stroke its neck. She was happy then. The evidence was visible in childhood photographs. After she married, the corners of her mouth started to turn down.

Now standing in the room of her youth, I realize that my parents influenced my life, positively and negatively. Both had their own sets of circumstances to deal with. Finally, I could see them as two human beings who did the best they could.

We all have our own breaking point. Mine was my sterility. Perhaps Dad's downfall came from trying to live up to Mom's expectations while she couldn't conform to his Bohemian lifestyle which first attracted her.

Uncle Mort called me out of my daydream and pulled me back to the present. He reminded me of my mother and I was glad Linda was able to meet him and experience the same gentle nature my mother had.

When it was time to leave, I watched as my daughter and my uncle clung to each other and wept. I think Uncle Mort must have seen the beautiful woman who had missed being part of the

family he loved so much. He wasn't just welcoming her into the family, rather he displayed a deep need fulfilled, an awareness of a cherished child returned home. It was their hello and their goodbye. He died shortly thereafter.

CHAPTER 28

MOTHER'S DAY. PETER was busy delivering coffee in bed to the two mothers of the house. Then we were off to Horst's and Cecile's.

I snapped photographs as Linda sat on the grass by Cecile's flower garden. Laughing, I told her I needed to buy lots of fridge magnets to accommodate so many new family pictures. I imagined her as the Mona Lisa in Monet's garden. She was all of the great masterpieces in one. Her voice brought to mind Beethoven or Mozart, each happy sound danced in my mind as I, a Virgin Mother, experienced my first Mother's Day.

I had sat under my tree in Vancouver before coming here and I prayed to find the perfect Mother's Day gift for my daughter, one that would accurately express my feelings. I knew exactly what I wanted and didn't quit searching until I found it - a statue of a mother and child. It was a circle with the face of mother and daughter facing each other at the top. There

was no beginning, nor end to their bodies, just a look of love as they stared into each others eyes.

Finding the perfect card was much more difficult. Each card I picked up expressed joyful memories of childhood. With great pain, I put them back on the shelf one by one until I found a card with a huge baby towering over its mother. My baby was twenty-seven after all! I signed it, Love M.

M was my signature for memos at work. It stood for Margaret but I confessed to Linda that in her case, it was my secret abbreviation for Mom. She referred to me as Margaret and I knew she couldn't and shouldn't refer to me as her mother. Peter, however, tried to make up for this by calling me Mom right from the start.

Linda's gift to me was a photograph of herself, in an old fashioned ceramic frame covered in soft pink roses. It was of her at age three feeding squirrels. She said she had something else, but wanted to wait until we got back to her house to share it with me.

That evening, she sat me down in Peter's Lazy Boy chair while she put on a CD. It was Michelle Wright's 'He Would Be

Sixteen.'

"I can't believe you've never heard this song," she said. "It always made me think of you."

I sat quietly as the music began to play.

She gets in her car,
October Friday night,
Home from work down 31,
past Franklin High,
She can see the stadium lights
she can hear the bell
A thousand crazy kids screaming in the stands,

What about the homecoming queen?
Love too young to know what it means
She goes back in time all in her mind
It's like a dream
He would be sixteen

Linda watched me, her eyes moist. "The words make me cry," she said.

The son she never knew
It hurt so much to give him up
but what else could she do?
He would be sixteen.

A child should have a home
She knows her folks were right

"Oh, Mom," my words escaped involuntarily. My mother had tried to do what was best.

Linda and I sat across from each other and cried together

as we listened to the words.

She never heard the couple's name
Just that they were nice.

Our eyes locked.

She wonders if he's tall
as his father was?
Does he drive a car by now?
Has he been in love?

She shakes back to reality
She knows things turned out the way they should
Be but she just can't help but ask herself
Does he know about me?

He would be sixteen the son she never knew.
It hurt so much to give him up but what else
Could she do
He would be sixteen.

She never even got to hold him
and nights like this
it hurts so much to miss
the son she's never seen.

He would be sixteen.

Sitting on the edge of the lazy boy, my daughter held me as I wept over the lyrics, my story in music. "Thank you for having me," she whispered.

THE FOLLOWING DAY, Linda arranged for me to meet her

childhood friends before we visited her parents. We were both nervous.

Kelly lived a few blocks from Linda's parents. They'd been friends since grade school. When I entered her home, there was a festive feeling as several women stood to greet us.

"We went to the University of Montreal together one summer to study French," a petite brunette of Arabic ancestry told me.

"So did I," Kelly added.

"Sounds like you majored in partying and spoke little French." I said. They nodded in agreement.

"The last night of the summer, a group of us went to the top of Mont Royal and ordered pizza from a phone booth. And the restaurant delivered it to a picnic area beside the road!"

Each had her own tale to relate, such as the story about Linda's first date, a geek that no one liked. She had been teacher's pet in grade eight, the year she permed her hair 'beyond friz'.

"We went to Niagara Falls one weekend and picked up an entire baseball team," her friend, Christie, told me.

Each bragged in some way, causing my dear sweet girl to blush and laugh and cry. These were the girls in the video Peter had made me. They all said the right things, telling me how much we looked alike, insisting I was too young to be a grandmother. With only sixteen years between us, we were more like sisters.

WE LEFT AT six o'clock to have dinner with Linda's parents. I experienced an odd combination of jealousy, fear and curiosity as we pulled up in front of their house, a pleasant suburban bungalow overlooking a ravine. So, this was where my daughter grew up. It was certainly nicer than anything I could have given her.

“Mom and Dad have done a lot of renovations since I was little,” Linda told me as we mounted the steps to ring the bell.

The door opened and there they were, the people who raised my daughter. Linda hugged her parents, then turned to introduce us.

"Mom, Dad, this is Margaret. Margaret, these are my parents, Wilda and Harold." Pride filled her words as she looked at each of us in turn. She reminded me of a little girl showing off

her new shiny marbles, convinced she had the best in the world.

Wilda's hair was gray. She was a little stocky, looking a bit older than her sixty-two years. She wore glasses and had a sternness to her face that Linda lacked. Her adoptive father stood silently beside his wife.

"Come in," her mother motioned.

She led us into the living room. It was large with silver wallpaper with swirls of a slightly different silver running through it.. Sliding glass doors led to the patio, overlooking the lush green ravine, reminding me of The Bush where I grew up and had spent so many happy hours exploring as a kid.

I sat on their gray leather couch. A bottle of wine had been set out in an ice bucket. Her father poured me a glass. The music of Glen Gould, a Bach piano concerto, played in the background.

I observed a wave of jealously, a tightening of my chest but pushed the feeling aside. Stay focused on how nice her parents are, I scolded myself. They didn't have to share Linda with me. Remember, it must be difficult for them, also.

"Cheers." We raised our glasses and drank.

"Would you like to see Linda's room?" her mother asked.

"Yes, I would love to."

Standing outside Linda's bedroom, Wilda said, "I haven't changed a thing since she moved out. It's exactly as it was when she lived here." She smiled, revealing her pride in having given her daughter everything she could. "Linda wanted white, so white it was."

It amazed me that she was so willing to have me in her daughter's life. I'm not sure I would have been so generous. She could have responded differently and chosen not to tell Linda about my ad. It was impossible not to feel love for her as we stood in our daughter's childhood room.

"I have a box of mementos that I kept of her school days if you would like to see it?"

"Of course."

Back downstairs, her mother reminisced as she pulled out old report cards, sports day ribbons and childish homemade cards which said, 'I love you Mommy' surrounded in hearts. Once more I had to consciously push the jealousy away.

"Would you like the extras?" Wilda asked, holding out

partial sheets of school photographs from various years. Each sheet had pictures cut out. I imagined my daughter had swapped pictures with girlfriends and perhaps a few boys.

"Oh, yes. I'd like that very much." I patted her hand. "Thank you."

She regarded my hand on hers for a brief moment then pulled away and began to cut off copies for me.

I carefully placed the photographs in my purse. "I'll put them in a collage frame like the one you have, Linda, and put it in my den."

Wilda pulled a photograph album from the shelf and watched me as I turned the pages of my daughter's life. There were photos of various Christmases showing a tree overflowing with gifts and a young Linda's face etched with excitement. I thought briefly of the twenty seven Christmases listening to The First Noel played over and over in shops and on the radio and how my heart would break with missing her. How my body ached to hold my baby. I closed my eyes briefly and remembered crying endlessly wondering whether she was alive or dead.

"We're happy that you and Linda have met, but," Wilda

turned to her daughter, "don't forget it was me who held you at night when you were sick and worried if you were out late." She was letting me know that she was Linda's real mother. I was merely the woman who gave birth to her.

Her father brought out a cassette tape, which he had copied for me. It was of Linda singing Merry Christmas when she was four. The rest of the tape contained classical music.

"Mom is an accomplished pianist." Linda said proudly. She held Cassandra on the piano bench, her little fingers pressed on the keys. We all agreed that perhaps Cassandra would follow in her grandmother's footsteps. And her great grandmother's, I thought, imagining my mother smiling down on Cassandra at the piano.

At dinner, Wilda looked at me and then at Linda and announced authoritatively, "You don't look at all alike."

"Really," Linda said, surprised. I knew better than to press it. She needed to imagine us as different. Linda shrugged and winked at me.

"I've always wondered how an ugly duckling like me could have had such a beautiful baby," her mother continued,

and I realized that neither of us felt as though we deserved the gift of Linda. I felt her suffering. We were both her mother and not her mother.

Dinner was turkey and I mentioned to Wilda how Linda had bragged about her mother's stuffing. And indeed it was delicious.

Over dessert, her mother grew serious. Dishes cleared, coffee poured, she put her arms on the table, lit a cigarette and started her interrogation.

"Was your father mean to you as a little girl? Was there incest?" The directness of her questions surprised me. Linda caught my eye and looked concerned. I paused to consider whether I should answer. I didn't believe she had the right to ask but she was regarding me with such intensity. I didn't want to destroy what had been a lovely evening and perhaps she deserved answers about her daughter's family history.

"No. There was no incest. I know some women grow up and suddenly remember sexual abuse, but I'm certain it never happened to me.

"Did he beat you?"

"He never laid a hand on me."

"But he drank, I'm told."

"Yes. He was a drinker." She continued her probe. I tried to answer patiently. She asked about my mother and even my drinking habits. She drilled me for a good hour. Linda fidgeted while her father sat quietly. I continued to answer as honestly as I could while constantly fighting the urge to cut her off.

As we were leaving, I thanked them again and again, searching for words that would convey the depth of my gratitude for sharing their daughter with me and making our reunion possible.

"You don't have to keep thanking us all the time," her mother responded.

Harold, however, stood quietly at the door and held my hands, his eyes locked mine with an intensity that revealed his feelings. We seemed to have reached inside each other's hearts and understood the magnitude of what we had been destined to share. The gift of his Linda to me, and of my Noel to him. Despite how little we had spoken that evening, our one meaningful glance bound us on a deep spiritual level. I will never forget that

moment and the love I felt generating from him.

On the drive back to Milton, Linda explained that her mother had taken a psychology course and believed she could psychoanalyze people. She apologized for her directness but thanked me for handling it so well.

I confessed I had felt uncomfortable but I didn't think Wilda was trying to dissect me, but rather she wanted to know where her daughter had come from. After all, she had built this wonderful story that I was a nice girl who had to give up her baby and now she wanted to confirm it for herself.

Linda shrugged. She started to say something about her mother's questions being inappropriate but stopped. I didn't push. Most kids were easily embarrassed by their parents, I thought. Certainly David's girls had let us know often enough when they didn't approve of our behavior.

THE NON-IDENTIFYING PAPERS from Children's Aid sat on the table between us. The government agency arranged reunions between adoptive children and birth parents only if both parties registered. Linda had registered to meet me the previous

summer. Because I had moved since registering on her twenty-first birthday, the letter informing me that my daughter wanted to connect with me was returned. Therefore, without my express consent, she only qualified to receive information regarding her birth family which didn't reveal who I was. It had taken this long for the government to respond to her request. I curled up on the couch to read their assessment of me at sixteen and was amazed to discover how accurate the information was.

The background history from Children's Aid was prefaced with an informative description of the times:

> ***The social climate up to and throughout the 1960's offered little acceptance for the woman bearing a child out of wedlock. It was not uncommon for a birth mother to be sent from home to a different city, without the support of friends and family. She was not encouraged to talk of her experience, to see her newborn baby or to consider the option of parenting the child herself.***
>
> ***She learned little of the adoptive family and was not aware of the adoptive family and not aware of the placement or the finalization of the Adoption Order. For many birth mothers, the shame and guilt attached to the pregnancy caused continual pain and anguish for years afterwards.***

Boy, they got that right!

> ***Your birth mother was described as being a mature, attractive girl who spoke easily about herself when alone in the interview with the worker from the Children's Aid Society. She seemed independent and very capable of making her own decisions.***

She was co-operative and demonstrated a courteous manner. Her interests were intellectual and cultural rather than athletic. She was interested in architecture and psychology. She enjoyed riding horses and preferred solitude rather than a crowd.

She was hoping that you would be adopted by a family who had religious faith. She believed deeply in God, but church worship was not necessary to her beliefs.

Your birth mother gave her situation a good deal of thought and consideration, and although she had very deep feelings for you, she knew that she could not possibly provide you with the things that an adoptive family could. She wanted you to have the stability and security of two warm and loving adoptive parents and hoped that you would be given many opportunities to live a very happy and fulfilling life. She gave the worker a verse which she was anxious for your adoptive parents to have, as it expressed her hope for you, as you were born on a Sunday.It reads as follows,

"Monday's child is fair of face,
Tuesday's child is full of grace,
Wednesday's child is loving and giving,
Thursday's child works hard for a living,
Friday's child is full of woe,
Saturday's child has far to go,
But the child that is born on the Sabbath Day
Is brave and bonny, good and gay.

Linda told me that she never went to church as a child, nor was exposed to any religion. I was angry that Children's Aid had not honored my single request but I had to admit that my daughter seemed perfectly well balanced just the same.

I CALLED JEFF from the airport before I left on Tuesday morning. The situation was worse than I expected. Monica came to his office the afternoon we had lunch together. His secretary, Pearl, had raved about meeting my daughter. Monica became so incensed his secretary had been told about my past that she stormed out of the office and went home and packed her things. Because I took my daughter to meet her uncle! She came home eventually, but he had to inform me of the seriousness of the situation. She was forcing him to choose.

ON THE PLANE, I sat back and reflected on my time with Linda and her family. The highlight was our goodbye. I had stood at the top of the stairs ready to carry my luggage to the car when Linda stopped to hug me. It was then that she first told me she

loved me.

Standing there, I held her and cherished those three words which made everything that happened to me worthwhile. Kissing the top of her head, I had said, 'I love you too. Really love you. Not just the dream of Noel but the reality of who you are today. You're a remarkable woman.'

Standing at the top of the stairs holding each other, I wondered if perhaps she needed me as much as I needed her. Perhaps she felt as lucky to find me as I felt to have found her. David assured me that anyone would be thrilled to discover me as their mother, but until she uttered those three words, I had not felt worthy.

Linda understood that loving me didn't imply she loved her parents less. She knew she had enough love to embrace us all. I wished Monica could understand the human capacity for love.

SORTING THE MAIL a few days later, I recognized Linda's writing immediately and ripped open her card. A baby was pictured on the cover. She had written Margaret then crossed it off and wrote Mom instead.

Dearest ~~Margaret~~ Mom,
I know you missed this stage of my life (on the cover of the card). I will try to fill you in on it as best possible. I thank you from the bottom of my heart for the life you gave me. It means everything to me to know you now. I feel I really love you and was always bonded in some way to you over the last 27 years. Please enjoy Cassandra and the next baby as much as possible. They are my only gift to you for the gift of life you gave me.
I love you,
Noel
xoxoxo

My heart skipped a beat when I saw that she called me Mom and signed Noel. I knew it was a conscious gift on her part and most likely wouldn't happen in a real conversation, but I cherished it even if just for a private moment on paper.

CHAPTER 29

"HI, "HIS VOICE was soft over the phone. I pushed my cat off my lap and sat up.

"Jeff! What a surprise." He had not called me since he told Monica about my reunion with Linda. "How are you?"

"Okay, I guess." His words were slurred.

"You sound as though you've been drinking."

"I'm in the bar with my friend, John. We've been talking about your daughter. He's very happy for you."

"I always liked that guy."

"Yeah, well, we've been talking and I just want to say," his voice was so quiet I could barely hear him, "I love you."

"I love you, too. I have from the moment you were born. Nothing can ever change that." I paused. "I really need my family to accept each other."

"I'll work on Monica."

"Thanks. And Jeff."

"Yes."

"Don't drink too much, okay."

SO THERE IT was. The duality of my brother. The nice guy and the obedient husband. It seems everyone has two sides. There were two sides to my Dad, the drinker and the dreamer. My mother hid her anger behind a sweet, shy facade.

Then there was me. I kept my secret self-hidden and spent years cultivating a strong public image. What I noticed now, was that every time I exposed my past, a little more of the pain dissolved.

"MONICA CALLED ME at the office today," David told me when he got home after work the following day. "She demanded that we not phone Jeff anymore." He held his hand in the air to stop my protest. "She claims that he gets drunk after we call."

"What did you say?"

"I told her that if he drank, it had nothing to do with us. Then I asked why she hated us. You are not going to like her

response. She said, quote, unquote, 'It's that bastard child.' "He paused while the words sank in. I was too stunned to speak. "I told her that she was sick and needed psychiatric help and hung up on her. I'm sorry, Margie, I've probably ruined any chance of reconciliation but, I've never heard anyone talk like that before. The bastard child! It was truly evil."

CHAPTER 30

"DAVID," I YELLED excitedly into the phone, "Linda's gone to the hospital. She's overdue and they decided to induce labor."

"I'm sure Peter will call right away with any news."

And he did. They had a healthy baby boy. My new grandson. I knew it!

September 20, 2005

Dearest Mitchell,

What a gift you are to all of us. What a gift you are from your Mother to me. What a gift for your grandparents. And of course a gift to your dear mother and father and sister. But to me you shall always be one very special boy. To know you from birth. It is the biggest miracle of all. I am so blessed. I saw a picture today that your father mailed along with your birth announcement in the newspaper. What a joy to see David's and my name mentioned along with all of your other grandparents. What a lucky boy you are to have so many people to love you. You look just like your dear father. How fortunate for him. Cassandra is a mirror image of your mother so it seems only proper that you look like him.

Your mother tells me that you are already full of your own unique personality. I look forward to meeting you face to face real soon and holding you and loving you to pieces your whole life through.

Welcome to the world, Mitchell!

Love Grandmama

THE SEA WAS turbulent on that cool September afternoon. Choppy waves tossed debris onto the beach. Logs that had escaped from tugboats booms floated dangerously, hidden by the white caps. I stood in Stanley Park with wet hair and my clothes blowing wildly and watched the water crash into the seawall. I loved days like these. Leaning against my mother's tree, I felt its strength.

I had come to talk to my mother. To tell her about Mitchell. My prayers for a baby boy were answered.

I planned fly to Toronto and meet Mitchell the following week. Linda also insisted I visit at Christmas. It would be the first time I truly acknowledged the season, since my mother died on Christmas day in 1978. My First Noel, now that was something worth celebrating.

I allowed the rain and wind to envelop me as I prayed my thanks for the way my life was unfolding. I pictured my new

grandson and smiled. Turning my face towards the heavens, my tears mixed with raindrops as I called out, "I got him, Mom and Dad. I got my baby boy."

I felt my heart lift, like the wings of an eagle spread wide, grand and expansive. My past belonged to another time, a memory like a tiny leaf tossed away in the breeze. As the wind howled and the sea splashed over the walkway, the word I searched for popped into my consciousness: Kundalini, supercharged energy, a spiritual, mystical experience, an awakening with psychic, creative awareness.

All was as it should be.

25 YEARS LATER

It's been twenty-five years since I first met Linda. When I pulled this manuscript out of storage recently, I finally felt ready to share my experience.

I blinked and Cassandra and Mitchell are all grown up. My pregnancy and giving Linda up for adoption has become part of their history and I wonder how my story will impact their choices. Linda sat them both down as teenagers and told them that even though our reunion worked out well, they should never consider being a teenage parent. They seldom call me GRANDmama, only if they want something badly enough. Not just beautiful, but smart kids. They know what works.

Cassandra is engaged and we will most likely be great grandparents in a few years. Tyler is a delightful young man who calls his mother every day. Who wouldn't love a boy like that!

During the first three years, Linda and I remained a few

feet off the ground but gradually life came down to earth. Now she readily rolls her eyes at me or breathes an impatient breathe at what she deems a silly sentiment. Sometimes I wish we could have stayed in the intoxicating fascination stage forever.

I recently went hiking at Capilano Canyon. Walking through the rainforest, I realized it was a metaphor for my life:

Beginning at Cleveland Dam, its water free falling, like my emotions when I gave my baby away and again later when first Doug, then my mother died. Falling endlessly. The resulting mist, where the water hit bottom, shrouded the surroundings like my truth hidden for so many years. My emotions like old growth decomposed while young saplings clung precariously to the rock face, survival its intent. Glancing backwards until finally, I turned a corner and could no longer see the falls, my past hidden. Then my beautiful Linda-Noel entered my life. The steep cliffs, dark and imposing, opened up. The forest became lush and vibrant with life. The river widening naturally as it flows towards the ocean, a new vista, wide and expansive, endless opportunities, new horizons, new possibilities. I visited the fish hatcheries and watched the salmon struggle upstream to spawn. The

reproductive instinct was so strong. I identified with those female fish who fought so hard to give birth.

Sadly, Linda and Peter have divorced but she is now with Tom, a wonderful man who adores her as much as she should be adored. He's great with the kids and darn good looking as well.

Linda still calls me Margaret rather than mother, but that's okay. I rarely think of her as Noel. I'm quite content with Linda. We have developed a different sort of bond which is unique to us. We have taken trips together to mark special birthdays, India, Europe, Brazil, Vegas. So many happy shared memories for us both.

My niece, Virginia, once asked her mother why she hated Auntie Margaret. Monica answered, "This is a moral house. We don't discuss those things here." She doesn't seem to realize that the more she rejected me, the more Virginia was fascinated by her mysterious aunt and at twenty-three, is more like me than anyone else in the family. Jeff left his wife a few years ago. He has a terrific relationship with Linda and a special bond with my grandson, Mitchell, a fireman, who hangs out with him for a beer and to watch football.

The important people in my life, David and his family have embraced my daughter and that's all that matters to me. These past twenty-four years have included the sort of joys and struggles that many families encounter. David got cancer and looking back on those difficult months of his treatment and recovery, I recognize how frightened I was, not able to endure the thought losing another person I loved, but it's been sixteen years and although the doctors say he is out of danger, I don't think anyone who has been touched by cancer ever feels totally safe again. He is my rock and I am fortunate to share my life with someone who loves me as much as I love him.

The Sixties were a time of transition when society went through a period of great upheaval. Most families didn't discuss secrets. That's just the way it was. Young people started to confront things and questioned values, demanding their opinions be heard and logical answers given instead of accepting what they were told. If I had become pregnant a few years later, I'm certain my life would have turned out differently.

My parents did what they thought was best. Perhaps they felt it kinder to hide me close at hand rather than send me alone to a home for unwed mothers. There was no right or wrong. I just wish now that I had been I kinder daughter.

I'm one of the fortunate ones. Our reunion turned out well. I could never have revealed my past if I had not met Linda. This is my story. It is everything to me and yet in the larger scheme of life, my drama means nothing. It's just my story. And in the telling, there is a release.

These days, I wonder if the pendulum has swung too far with birth mothers choosing who adopts their child. If I had known where my baby was, I could never have surrendered emotionally and gotten on with my life. And her dear parents would never have been able to relax into being her mom and dad.

If I had a pregnant, sixteen year old daughter, would I make her give up her baby? I'm not sure. Morality is different and money is not a problem. I wouldn't wish the pain I suffered on anyone. I might do what many families did back then, pretend the baby was mine and raise it as a sibling of his or her mother.

I know what a gift my daughter was to her parents and how she filled a void in their life. Her mother and father died tragically in a car accident. I didn't know how to help Linda cope with her grief so I enrolled us in the same program I took when my mother died. EST, now called the Landmark Forum, was still controversial but the insights I gained had served me well over the past twenty-three years so I registered us together six months after her parents were killed.

Spending a weekend dedicated to considering personal issues, with my daughter in the room, was a profound experience. It gave me insight into my story in ways I had never considered. As for Linda, that's her story to tell.

I realized that everything about my persona has stemmed from losing my daughter. I am sixty-eight and since I was sixteen, I have distanced myself from people so that they never got close enough to learn about my past. I controlled all aspects of my life because I could not control the major event of 1966. I don't

delegate because I can do it better. I guess I'm still trying to prove my self-worth, despite my accomplishments.

I never allowed anyone to tell me what to do. I blamed my parents for forcing me to give up my daughter. However, I had stood up to them on other issues even as a young girl. If I had wanted to keep my daughter, I would have.

I finally came to understand that no one forced me to give up my baby. By giving my daughter both a mother and a father, I was being the best mother I could be.

ACKNOWLEDGEMENTS

Just as in food products which list the major ingredients, first, I must give my special gratitude to David and Linda.

David for never being embarrassed or secretive about my story- only joyfully sharing and encouraging me.

Linda for being fully in my life and loving me. For presenting her babies as a gift in her attempt to make up for not knowing her as she grew.

For her dear parents, Wilda and Harold, who shared her with me when they didn't have to and who have gone now but will forever remain in my heart.

A special thanks to my official listeners, Jeannette Malone and Larisa Broyde who assisted me throughout the years of rewrites. And to my editor and friend, Jessica Morrell of Independent Writing and Editing Professional in Portland.

To all my friends at Eileen Kernaghan's Port Moody writing group who endured the many rewrites and tears yet continued to encourage me.

For all my family and friends who welcomed Linda-Noel into the family and shared in my joy.

Made in the USA
San Bernardino, CA
06 March 2018